Caprial & John's Kitchen

Caprial & John's Kitchen

recipes for cooking together

Caprial & John Pence

Food photography by **Maren Caruso**

Ten Speed Press
Berkeley | Toronto

To all the staff at the cooking school and the Bistro:
thank you for all of your help in making everything
such a success.

       Caprial

To Alex and Savannah: in my life and career I have
acccomplished many things, and the two of you are
the best by far.

       Love, Dad

🔟
Ten Speed Press
P.O. Box 7123
Berkeley, California 94707
www.tenspeed.com

Distributed in Australia by Simon and Schuster Australia, in Canada by Ten Speed Press Canada, in New Zealand by Southern Publishers Group, in South Africa by Real Books, and in the United Kingdom and Europe by Airlift Book Company.

Food photography by Maren Caruso
Photo assistance by Faiza Ali
Food and prop styling by Erin Quon and Kim Konecny
Photographs on pages v, vi, ix, 31, 59, 78, 85, 90, 92, 111, 130, 161, 168, and 179 by Jerry Hart
Photographs on pages ii, viii, x, 3, 4, 13, 25, 26, 42, 109, 122, 137, 144, 152, 156, 180, and 190 by Susan Seubert, Portland, Oregon

Developmental editing and writing assistance by Jennifer Morrison
Book design by Nancy Austin

Library of Congress Cataloging-in-Publication Data
Pence, Caprial.
  Caprial and John's kitchen: partner cooking at
   home/Caprial and John Pence.
     p. cm.
  ISBN 1-58008-488-5 (alk. paper)
   1. Cookery. 2. Menus. I. Title: Caprial and John's
   kitchen. II. Pence, John, 1961– III. Title.
TX652.P42 2003
541.5--dc21

                2002032256

First printing, 2003
Printed in China

1 2 3 4 5 6 7 8 9 10 — 07 06 05 04 03

Contents

Acknowledgments

To our wonderful staff: thank you for all your hard work and pride in the restaurant and cooking school.

To Doe: thank you for all your support and expertise in putting this book together.

To Jenny: As always, you're the best; we would have been lost without you. Thanks for putting up with us all summer.

To all the wonderful photographers who worked on the book: Susan, Maren, and Jerry. Thank you for making the book so beautiful.

To Windy, Aaron, Nancy, and Lorena: thank you for your support and work making the book.

A special thank you to John, Mark, and Traci for keeping our world together and running smoothly.

Preface

Our life together began in the kitchen and has always been surrounded by the world of food. Although John and I are professional chefs, with our livelihood based on our restaurant and cooking school, it's the way cooking intertwines with our home life that matters most to us. After working with food all day, we gladly come home and cook again, to prepare a meal for our family and often friends, too. The menu might include a recipe we are testing for a cooking class or an upcoming cookbook, and we welcome the willing taste-testers. Together in the kitchen at home, with those we love lending a hand or just keeping us company, we get to truly relax and enjoy cooking—reminding us why we got into it in the first place.

The love of cooking was sparked in each of us when we were young. Raised in small-town New Jersey with his grandparents under the same roof, John was inspired by his grandmother, a skilled bread-baker and amazing home cook who prepared the family meals. Meanwhile, on the opposite side of the country, I grew up in a more globally influenced kitchen, as my parents were intrigued by the foods of various ethnicities and nationalities. John and I later met as students at the Culinary Institute of America (CIA), in New York's Hudson Valley. Introduced by a mutual friend, we attended a school-sponsored vegetable-carving demonstration on our first date and learned to sculpt garnishes like cucumber fish and radish crabs. Such fanciful touches never actually made their way into our cooking, but the date sealed our relationship.

We graduated in 1984 and headed in opposite directions for our first jobs: John to David's Country Inn in New Jersey, and I to the Shoalwater Restaurant on the southern coast of Washington. We handled being apart for about six months, and then got engaged and moved together to Seattle. We landed jobs at separate restaurants and immersed ourselves in the city's food scene, which

had a young, energizing vibe. It was an exciting time, with a resurgence of regional cuisine shaping the way people thought about food. John then began a starting position as a line cook at Fullers restaurant in the Sheraton Hotel, the hot spot for nouveau cuisine. In a quickly evolving saga, he was laid off a short time later, hired the next day for another job, and then called by Fullers the day after that and informed that his job was once again available. He declined the offer but suggested that they talk to his fiancée, and so I was hired. When a second line cook position opened a few months later, John was ready to apply. The restaurant's management was initially skeptical about having a couple working together on the line, but we convinced them to give it a try.

While the CIA provided us with a solid culinary education based in classic French training, working the line at Fullers gave us equally invaluable on-the-job experience. Now married, we were the youngest of an international crew that included chefs from Vietnam, Malaysia, El Salvador, and China. We were constantly learning from these skilled cooks who were seasoned by years in the industry, and who soon became like family. Outside of work, we got together to delve into different types of cooking and spent time preparing meals together in one another's homes. The international perspective still shapes our cooking today, and it is reflected in this book, our menu at the Bistro, and the recipes we teach.

After exploring just about everything there was to learn on the line at Fullers, we were ready for more challenges and responsibilities. John moved up in the culinary world when he was offered a chef position at another restaurant and jumped at the opportunity to run a kitchen. At Fullers, I made my way to lead chef, and then sous chef, and finally chef in 1987. An unbelievable amount of energy goes into running a restaurant, and we each put in 60 to 70 hours a week. Although we were absorbed by our work, we truly missed being colleagues in the kitchen. We stayed creatively connected by filling our days off with shopping at the Public Market and throwing dinner parties for our friends.

Life moved along at a steady clip. John went on to cook in other restaurants around town, building his connections in the industry. Fullers continued to gain national prominence, so I spent much of my time involved in the demands of public relations. In the midst of it all, our son, Alex, was born. Two demanding careers coupled with a baby—in spite of having a nanny—began to add an undeniable element of stress, so I proposed that John quit work to stay home and care for Alex. John became a champion of all things domestic, keeping Alex very happy while keeping the house under control, the garden beau-

tiful, and the champagne opened and dinner ready when I walked through the door at night. The domestic bubble burst about a year later when I came home and discovered a "crafty" John making candles. It was a clear sign that he was ready to get back into his own career. John began taking part-time positions in kitchens around town, and his experience and connections really paid off. He'd lend a hand wherever one was needed, by consulting on menu development, working the line if someone was sick, or providing support to newly opened restaurants.

We were considering opening our own place when a group of people approached us to join them in starting a restaurant. We loved the idea of working together again, but as it came close to making the partnership official, we decided against it. At the same time, Fullers' management

heard that I wanted to leave. When they asked why, I explained that John and I missed working together. Consequently, they offered to bring John on as co-chef, and again we found ourselves working side-by-side, this time running the kitchen together.

However, pleased as we were, we couldn't shake the notion of owning our own restaurant. A year later, my mother, a freelance bookkeeper in Portland, let us know that one of her clients was putting their small neighborhood restaurant and wine shop on the market. It was the perfect opportunity, so we bought it. Alex was just turning four and our second child, Savannah, was on the way, and we wanted to slow down a bit and get back some of that time together as a family, with the support of our extended family nearby. Once the Westmoreland Bistro and Wine (which we later renamed Caprial's Bistro and Wine) was ours, it was clear that owning our own restaurant was a lot more work than we had imagined it would be. Even so, with all of the responsibilities and worries, we were exactly where we wanted to be.

At the Bistro, we took turns cooking alongside our chef, yet it took us some time to get a sense of how to divide the other duties. Eventually things just naturally evolved according to our strengths and interests: John, a numbers guy with a vision of the big picture, gravitated toward the overall administration of the restaurant; I conceptualized the menu, met with wine purveyors, and worked the floor. We began teaching cooking classes together in the restaurant—something we had always wanted to do— but since the space was so small, we could only hold classes when the restaurant was closed. We were grateful for the positive response. Many of our students told us how they got a kick out of learning in such a relaxed fashion, watching us cook together and good-naturedly tease each other. They also said that they could relate to how it might be to work together with a spouse, and many identified with our sense of humor and give-and-take.

My career branched off into a television show and cookbooks, and demands on my time took me away from the daily business at the restaurant. Meanwhile, John transitioned into general manager. We hired a close friend to oversee the day-to-day operations, and our two chefs kept the kitchen under control. We were very pleased with how our business was growing, but we weren't thrilled with how often we were apart. Once again, we looked for a way to tie our careers and lives back together on a daily basis. Working together on the show was the answer, and our first series together aired in 2001.

In January 2002, we expanded our classes into a fullfledged cooking school, Caprial and John's Kitchen, complete with a host of guest chefs and a shop stocked with kitchenware, cookbooks, wine, and specialty ingredients. With an eye on the future, we designed the school so that it could double as a set for taping our cooking show.

As we ventured into the next stage of our career, we felt it was the right time for us to truly team up in all facets of our work. This is the first cookbook we have written together, and I feel it embodies the way we cook together at home.

Welcome to our kitchen. Now let's get started!

—Caprial Pence

ix

Caprial & John's
Kitchen

Fleur de Sel

Introduction

Over the last ten years, together we have cooked, run a restaurant, built a cooking school, and raised a family. Separately we have created our own recipes for both the classroom and restaurants, but this is the first time we have actually sat down and written recipes side-by-side. Even though culinary bliss reigns in our house, there were times when we didn't agree on every little nuance of all the recipes—prompting John to give the book the working title *Compromising with Caprial.*

We wrote this book to share our philosophy of celebrating the table and spending time together creating in the kitchen. We in America should borrow a chapter from European families, who have long known how to slow down and come together at the end of the day. Our current culture of packed schedules and virtual communication leaves few opportunities to spend time with loved ones and talk to each other face-to-face. Cooking together opens the door to savoring not only what you cook but also the time you spend creating. It provides an ideal setting—and purpose—for sharing time with anyone you'd like to get closer to, whether a friend, spouse, child, neighbor, sibling, or parent. Our kids, who are entering those noncommunicative teen years and seem to have taken a vow of silence whenever we're around, are getting used to us dragging them into the kitchen to cook with us. Usually they first come with protest, but once the smells of the kitchen soften their resolve and break their bonds of silence, we are amazed at the conversations we have and the dinner that evolves. And when it's just the two of us in the kitchen, it may be the only time all day when we aren't surrounded by our business responsibilities. This is when we can focus on each other while chopping, slicing, sautéing, and finishing with a beautifully prepared meal.

No matter how independent you are, even if you can pull off the most complicated menus by yourself or if you are reluctant to share your cooking domain, we encourage you to welcome another chef into the kitchen. It may be a little rocky at first, but if you go into it with an open mind and follow our suggestions on sharing the workload, you'll be amazed at how fast cooking together becomes second nature. (Keep in mind, however, that the recipes in this book are easy enough for one person to prepare, so working with a partner is not an absolutely essential ingredient.)

To facilitate the timing and execution of the menus presented in the entrées and sides chapter, we've included tips on how to break down the workload between two cooks in the kitchen. After cooking together at home for so many years, we have developed a pattern when putting together a more involved meal, such as for a dinner party. One of us tends to prepare the dessert earlier in the day, while the other makes the appetizer later in the afternoon. We usually cook together side-by-side when we are making the main course. Preparing this course is the hardest one to coordinate timing-wise, especially for the home cook. In fact, our students tell us that their biggest source of stress is that crucial time when every dish is calling for attention and, working alone, there aren't enough hands. We chose to include timing tips just for this chapter because we felt it was the most important place to focus our extra direction. Our aim isn't to distinguish between head chef and line cook, but rather to promote fun and stress-free cooking between co-chefs working together.

In order to maintain an idyllic partnership in the kitchen, each chef has to be comfortable and feel like he or she is master of the domain. This means each person needs a comfortable place to prep and, if possible, the right-sized chef's knife, which can become an extension of his or her hand. At our house, we each have a place in the kitchen to call our own and our own favorite knife, thus resolving any conflicts over who's the messier cook.

Another key to kitchen harmony is communication. Just as it's done in the professional kitchen, we are constantly bantering back and forth about what's been prepped, what needs to be done next, or when we should start to cook the next dish. By keeping up the lines of communication, whether we are at home, taping the show, or teaching a class, we—and anyone watching—know exactly where we are in the preparation.

You can expand this culinary partnership by shopping together, either at your everyday grocery store or someplace more inspiring, such as a farmers' market or specialty store. This will allow you to jointly make decisions about seasonal ingredients, perhaps finding a special ingredient that you can add to your menu, and choosing the perfect wine for a finishing touch. For us, this is often the beginning of our creative process, when an idea transforms into a complete menu.

As we always teach our students, substitute ingredients in the recipes to take advantage of seasonal products or to suit your personal taste. The same goes for the menus in this book—don't be locked into our combinations of entrées and side dishes, because they are suggestions only. We hope you and your cooking partner will find inspiration in these recipes and take them and make them your own. Whether you follow the recipes word-for-word or just use them as a starting point, we hope you create the same joy in your kitchen that's always been a part of ours.

Appetizers and Soups

Feta-Artichoke Dip

Serves 6

2 cloves garlic, chopped
1 cup crumbled feta cheese
$^1/_4$ cup tahini paste
1 cup diced artichoke bottoms
Juice and finely grated zest of 1 lemon
$^1/_4$ cup extra virgin olive oil
2 teaspoons chopped fresh thyme or lemon thyme
Salt and freshly ground black pepper
Lemon zest, for garnish
Thyme sprigs, for garnish
Crostini (page 181) or Sesame Water Crackers (page 8),
　　as accompaniment

Combine the garlic, feta, tahini paste, artichoke bottoms, and lemon juice and zest in a food processor, and process until smooth. With the machine running, slowly add the oil, and process until smooth. Add the thyme, process to mix, then season to taste with salt and pepper.

Transfer the dip to a serving bowl, and garnish with strips of lemon zest and thyme sprigs. Serve at room temperature with crostini or homemade water crackers.

Cannellini Bean Bruschetta with Black Truffle Oil

Serves 6

CANNELLINI BEANS
$^3/_4$ cup dried cannellini beans
2 cups water, plus more as needed
2 tablespoons extra virgin olive oil
2 cloves garlic, minced
$^1/_3$ cup grated fontina cheese
1 teaspoon black truffle oil
Salt and freshly ground black pepper

BRUSCHETTA
18 ($^1/_4$-inch-thick) slices baguette
2 tablespoons extra virgin olive oil

1 bunch sage, for garnish

To prepare the beans, combine the beans and water in a saucepan over medium heat, bring to a boil, and cook, uncovered, until the beans are al dente (tender with a bit of a bite), about 45 minutes, adding additional water as needed. Add the olive oil and continue cooking until the beans are tender, about 10 minutes longer. Remove the pan from the heat, add the garlic and fontina, and mix until the cheese has melted. Add the truffle oil, mix well, and season to taste with salt and pepper. Keep warm.

To prepare the bruschetta, preheat the oven to 350°F. Arrange the bread slices on a sheet pan and drizzle with the olive oil. Bake for about 15 minutes, until toasted and golden brown.

To serve, place the warm beans in the center of a serving platter or tray, arrange the bruschetta around the beans, and garnish with sage leaves.

Smoked Eggplant Baba Ghanouj

Serves 6

2 large eggplant, halved vertically
3 cloves garlic, minced
1/3 cup tahini paste
Juice and finely grated zest of 1 lemon
2/3 cup extra virgin olive oil
1 teaspoon ground cumin
Salt
1/2 teaspoon Asian chile paste
2 teaspoons lemon olive oil (optional)
Pita bread or crostini (page 181), as accompaniment

To smoke the eggplant, remove the grill from the barbecue, and then prepare the coals by piling briquettes on one side of the barbecue and lighting them. Let them burn until they are gray in color, about 30 minutes. Place a handful of smoking chips (alder, apple, hickory, or any type of hardwood) on a square of aluminum foil, and place the foil on the hot coals. Oil the grill and set it back on the barbecue. Arrange the eggplant cut side down on the opposite side of the grill from the coals. Cover the barbecue and let the eggplant smoke until fork-tender, about 1 1/2 hours, adding more chips as needed to keep the smoke from dying down.

To make the baba ghanouj, scoop the eggplant from the skin (discard the skin) and combine in a food processor with the garlic and tahini. Process until very smooth. Add the lemon juice and zest, oil, and cumin, and process until smooth. Season to taste with salt.

To serve, spread the baba ghanouj on a large plate. Spoon the chile paste onto the center of the baba ghanouj, and drizzle with the lemon olive oil. Serve at room temperature with warm pita bread or crostini.

Wild Mushroom Flans

Serves 6

1 ounce dried porcini mushrooms
2 cups dry sherry
1 tablespoon extra virgin olive oil
1 large shallot, minced
2 cloves garlic, minced
2 3/4 cups heavy whipping cream
6 large egg yolks
1/2 teaspoon finely chopped fresh rosemary
1/2 teaspoon finely chopped fresh thyme
Salt and freshly ground black pepper

Preheat the oven to 300°F.

In a large bowl, cover the porcini with the sherry, and let it sit for about 20 minutes. When the mushrooms are soft and have absorbed most of the sherry, drain off and reserve any extra liquid. Coarsely chop the mushrooms.

Heat the oil in a large sauté pan over medium heat until hot. Add the shallot and garlic and sauté for about 1 minute. Add the mushrooms and toss well. Add the reserved porcini liquid and reduce until the mixture is almost dry, 2 to 3 minutes. Remove from the heat and let cool until tepid.

In a large mixing bowl, combine the mushroom mixture with the cream, egg yolks, rosemary, and thyme, and mix well. Season with salt and pepper.

Ladle the mixture into six 8-ounce ramekins. Place the ramekins in a shallow roasting pan, add enough hot water to reach about halfway up the sides of the ramekins, and set the pan in the oven. Bake the custards for 50 to 60 minutes, until just set or a knife inserted in the custards comes out clean. Remove the ramekins from the water bath. Serve warm.

Grilled Radicchio Stuffed with Goat Cheese

Serves 6

6 large radicchio leaves
6 ounces soft mild goat cheese
6 thin slices pancetta
**2 tablespoons high-quality balsamic vinegar
(aged at least 10 years)**

Oil the grill and prepare a medium-hot fire. If you are using a gas grill, preheat over medium heat. If you are using a charcoal grill, let the coals burn until they are covered with gray ash. The grill is medium-hot when you can hold your hand over the grill for no longer than 5 seconds.

While the grill is heating, prepare the radicchio leaves. Place one leaf on a flat work surface with the stem end closest to you. Place about 1 ounce of the goat cheese in the center of the leaf. Fold the stem end of the leaf over the filling. Fold the two sides over the filling, then roll up to form an egg roll shape. Wrap a slice of pancetta tightly around the radicchio and secure with two toothpicks. Repeat with the remaining radicchio, goat cheese, and pancetta until six rolls are formed.

Place the stuffed leaves on the grill and grill, turning often, until the pancetta is crispy, about 5 minutes. (Be sure to keep an eye on the fire so it doesn't flare up and burn the leaves.)

To serve, place the radicchio rolls on a serving platter or tray and drizzle with the vinegar. Serve warm.

Sesame Water Crackers

Makes 6 dozen crackers

3 cups all-purpose flour
1 teaspoon salt
1 cup warm (105° to 115°F) water
$^1/_2$ cup sesame seeds
Sea salt

Combine the flour and salt in a food processor. With the motor running, slowly add the water and process just until the dough forms on top of the blades. Remove the dough from the food processor and wrap it in plastic wrap; let it rest at room temperature for 1 hour.

Preheat the oven to 375°F (you will see the best results in a convection oven). Lightly grease a sheet pan.

Cut the dough into six equal pieces. Working with one piece at a time, roll the dough out on a well-floured board into a long, paper-thin cracker (the thinner the better). (If you prefer, you can use a pasta machine to roll the dough out as thinly as possible.) Carefully lay the cracker on the prepared pan, cutting it in half if it is too long to fit on the pan. Brush the cracker with water, then sprinkle with the sesame seeds and sprinkle lightly with sea salt. Using a pastry wheel, score the cracker vertically every inch or so.

Bake for about 8 minutes, until golden brown. Let cool for about 5 minutes on the pan, then remove from the pan and let cool completely. Continue rolling out and baking the remaining dough. Store in an airtight container for up to 3 days.

Eggplant and Tomato Tarts
with Olive Tapenade

Serves 6

6 ($^1/_2$-inch-thick) slices eggplant (about 1 medium
    eggplant)
2 teaspoons kosher salt
$^1/_4$ cup extra virgin olive oil
6 plum tomatoes, halved lengthwise
3 tablespoons good-quality balsamic vinegar
    (aged at least 5 years)
$^1/_2$ recipe Quick Puff Pastry (page 182)
1 large egg, beaten with 1 teaspoon water
$^1/_4$ cup crumbled blue cheese
Salt and freshly ground black pepper

OLIVE TAPENADE
1 cup kalamata olives, pitted
1 head garlic, roasted (see page 187)
1 $^1/_2$ teaspoons drained capers
2 tablespoons chopped fresh basil
$^1/_4$ cup extra virgin olive oil

Basil sprigs, for garnish

Preheat the oven to 375°F. Line a sheet pan with parchment paper.

To prepare the tart filling, toss the eggplant slices with the salt in a bowl, and let sit for about 10 minutes.

Meanwhile, heat 2 tablespoons of the oil in a large sauté pan over high heat until hot. Add the tomatoes, skin side down, and cook, without stirring, until brown, 3 to 4 minutes. Add the vinegar, cover the pan with a lid, and cook about 3 minutes longer. Transfer the tomatoes to a plate; set aside. Add the remaining 2 tablespoons oil to the pan and heat over high heat until hot. Add as many of the eggplant slices as will fit without overcrowding the pan and sear until golden brown, 2 to 3 minutes per side. Transfer the eggplant slices to a plate; set aside. Continue with the remaining eggplant.

To prepare the tarts, roll out the puff pastry on a well-floured board into an 8 by 12-inch rectangle. Cut the rectangle in half lengthwise to form two pieces, each 4 by 12 inches. Cut each piece into thirds to form six 4-inch squares. Place 1 pastry square on a flat work surface. Starting $^1/_2$ inch diagonally from one corner, use a sharp knife to make a 2 $^1/_2$-inch-long cut parallel to the edge of the pastry, stopping within 1 inch from the end. Next, beginning in the same corner as the original cut, make another 2 $^1/_2$-inch-long cut along the edge perpendicular to the original cut. Repeat the procedure in the opposite corner. You should end up with a partially cut square $^1/_2$ inch smaller than the 4-inch square of pastry. Brush the $^1/_2$-inch-wide strip of pastry with the egg wash, then carefully lift it at one corner and fold over to the opposite inner corner. Press to seal. Repeat with the opposite corner. Place the tart shells on the prepared sheet pan.

Divide the cooked tomatoes among the prepared tart shells, and top each tart with 1 slice of eggplant. Crumble the blue cheese over the eggplant slices and season with salt and pepper. Bake the tarts for about 25 minutes, until golden brown.

While the tarts are baking, prepare the tapenade. Combine the olives, garlic, capers, and basil in a food processor and process to chop. With the motor running, slowly add the oil, and process until incorporated.

To serve, place each tart on a plate, top with a bit of the tapenade, and garnish with a sprig of basil. Serve warm.

Spice-Rubbed Steak with Baked Tortilla Chips and Green Goddess Dressing

Serves 6

SPICY DRY RUB

1 tablespoon dark brown sugar

1 teaspoon ground cumin

$1/2$ teaspoon chile powder

$1/2$ teaspoon garlic powder

$1/2$ teaspoon onion powder

$1/4$ teaspoon cayenne pepper

2 (8-ounce) New York steaks

Salt

GREEN GODDESS DRESSING

1 tablespoon tarragon vinegar

1 clove garlic

1 large egg yolk

1 tablespoon freshly squeezed lemon juice

2 oil- or salt-packed anchovy fillets

$1/2$ teaspoon chopped fresh tarragon

$1/2$ tablespoon chopped fresh flat-leaf parsley

1 scallion, both white and green parts, minced

$3/4$ cup extra virgin olive oil

2 tablespoons sour cream

Salt and freshly ground black pepper

BAKED TORTILLA CHIPS

6 large flour tortillas, cut into 6 wedges each

1 tablespoon vegetable oil

1 $1/2$ teaspoons kosher salt

Flat-leaf parsley sprigs, for garnish

To prepare the dry rub, combine all the ingredients in a bowl and mix well. Rub the steaks with the spice mixture, then refrigerate the steak until you are ready to grill, up to 1 hour.

Oil the grill and prepare a hot fire. If you are using a gas grill, preheat over high heat. If you are using a charcoal grill, let the coals burn until they are covered with gray ash. The grill is hot when you can hold your hand over the grill for no longer than 2 seconds. Season the steaks with salt. Grill the steaks until they reach an internal temperature of 135°F, 3 to 4 minutes per side for medium doneness, depending on the thickness of the steaks. Let cool for 5 minutes, then refrigerate until well chilled, up to 24 hours.

To prepare the dressing, combine the vinegar, garlic, egg yolk, lemon juice, anchovies, tarragon, parsley, and scallion in a food processor, and process until well blended. With the motor running, slowly add the olive oil, and process until smooth. Transfer the mixture to a bowl, fold in the sour cream, and season to taste with salt and pepper. Refrigerate the dressing until you are ready to serve.

To prepare the tortilla chips, preheat the oven to 425°F. Place the tortilla wedges on a sheet pan, drizzle with the vegetable oil, and sprinkle with the kosher salt. Bake for 5 to 6 minutes, until golden brown.

To serve, slice the chilled steaks very thinly against the grain. Divide the tortilla chips among six plates. Distribute the steak slices over the tortilla chips and drizzle with the dressing. Serve immediately, garnished with parsley sprigs.

Crispy Risotto Fritters

Serves 6

5 cups cooked risotto (page 183), chilled
³/₄ pound fontina cheese, diced
¹/₄ cup chopped fresh basil
Vegetable oil for deep-frying
1 cup all-purpose flour
3 large eggs, beaten
3 cups fresh bread crumbs (page 181)
Basil sprigs, for garnish
Quick Tomato and Cured Olive Sauce (page 60),
as accompaniment, warmed

To shape the fritters, place about ¹/₃ cup of the cooked risotto in your hand and pat it into a 2- to 3-inch circle. Place a piece of the cheese in the center of the risotto and top with a pinch of basil. Form the risotto into a ball around the cheese; set aside. Continue with the remaining risotto, cheese, and basil to make about fifteen balls total.

Heat about 4 inches of oil in a heavy saucepan over high heat until it reaches 350°F. While the oil is heating, bread the fritters. Place the flour on a plate; the eggs in a large, shallow bowl; and the bread crumbs on another plate. Dredge the fritters in the flour, dip them in the egg, then coat well in the bread crumbs. When the oil is hot, add as many fritters as will fit in the pan without overcrowding, and fry until golden brown, about 3 minutes. Drain on paper towels. Continue with the remaining fritters.

To serve, place the fritters on a serving platter and garnish with basil sprigs. Serve hot, with warm tomato sauce on the side.

Black Pepper–Encrusted Scallops with Mint Yogurt Sauce

Serves 6

MINT YOGURT SAUCE
3/4 cup whole-milk yogurt
1 clove garlic, minced
1 tablespoon chopped fresh mint
1/2 teaspoon ground coriander
1/4 teaspoon ground cumin
Salt

PITA CRISPS
3 pita rounds, cut into 8 wedges each
1 tablespoon extra virgin olive oil
1 teaspoon sea salt

SCALLOPS
1 tablespoon freshly ground black pepper
18 sea scallops
Salt
1 tablespoon vegetable oil

Mint sprigs, for garnish

To prepare the sauce, combine the yogurt, garlic, mint, coriander, and cumin in a bowl, and whisk together. Season to taste with salt. Refrigerate until you are ready to serve.

To prepare the pita crisps, preheat the oven to 350°F. Arrange the pita wedges in a single layer on a sheet pan, then brush them with the olive oil, and sprinkle with the sea salt. Bake for 10 to 15 minutes, until crispy and golden brown.

To prepare the scallops, place the pepper on a small plate. Season the scallops with salt, then dredge them lightly in the pepper. Heat the vegetable oil in a very large sauté pan over high heat until smoking hot. Add the scallops and cook until just barely cooked through, about 1 minute per side.

To serve, arrange three scallops on each plate, drizzle with the sauce, and garnish with mint sprigs. Serve immediately with the pita crisps.

Steamed Mussels with Crème Fraîche

Serves 6

2 cloves garlic, chopped
2 shallots, chopped
1 cup dry white wine
2 tablespoons unsalted butter
1 tablespoon chopped fresh parsley
2 teaspoons chopped fresh tarragon
1 bay leaf
3 pounds fresh mussels, cleaned and debearded
3/4 cup crème fraîche (page 181)
Salt and freshly ground black pepper

Combine the garlic, shallots, wine, butter, parsley, tarragon, and bay leaf in a large stockpot over high heat, and bring to a boil. Add the mussels, cover, and cook, stirring once or twice, just until the mussels open, about 8 minutes. Discard any mussels that do not open. Using a slotted spoon, remove the mussels from the cooking liquid and divide them among six bowls. Set the pan back over high heat and reduce the cooking liquid until it lightly coats the back of a spoon, about 4 minutes. Add the crème fraîche, mix well, and season to taste with salt and pepper. Remove the bay leaf. To serve, spoon the hot sauce over the mussels. Serve hot.

Crab and Fresh Corn Cakes

Serves 6

1/2 onion, minced
2 cloves garlic, minced
1 1/2 cups fresh crabmeat
1 cup fresh corn kernels (about 1 ear)
2 large eggs, beaten
2 tablespoons cayenne sauce
1 tablespoon Dijon mustard
1 teaspoon Worcestershire sauce
1/2 cup all-purpose flour
1/2 cup finely ground cornmeal
1 tablespoon baking powder
Salt and freshly ground black pepper
2 tablespoons unsalted butter
1 bunch scallions, both white and green parts, thinly sliced, for garnish
2 limes, cut into wedges, for garnish

Combine the onion, garlic, crabmeat, and corn in a large bowl, and toss well. Add the eggs and mix well. Add the cayenne sauce, mustard, and Worcestershire sauce, and mix well. Add the flour, cornmeal, and baking powder, and mix just until the batter comes together. Season well with salt and pepper.

Heat the butter in a very large nonstick sauté pan or on a griddle over medium-high heat until melted and bubbling. Using a 2-ounce ladle, form as many cakes as will fit without overcrowding the pan, and cook until golden brown, 2 to 3 minutes per side. Transfer to a warm oven while continuing with the remaining batter.

To serve, place two cakes on each plate, and garnish with scallions and lime wedges. Serve immediately.

Pan-Fried Oysters with Spicy Pepper Relish

Serves 6

SPICY PEPPER RELISH
1 clove garlic, chopped
$^1/_4$ red onion, minced
1 Anaheim chile, minced
2 red jalapeño chiles, minced
Juice and finely grated zest of 1 lime
$^1/_4$ cup extra virgin olive oil
1 teaspoon chopped fresh cilantro
$^1/_2$ teaspoon ground cumin
Pinch of ground cinnamon
Salt

30 small oysters, such as yearlings, in the shell
2 large eggs
2 tablespoons water
4 cups all-purpose flour
1 cup finely ground cornmeal
1 teaspoon salt
1 teaspoon freshly ground black pepper
3 tablespoons extra virgin olive oil
Rock salt, for serving

Cilantro or flat-leaf parsley sprigs, for garnish

To prepare the relish, combine the garlic, onion, chiles, lime juice and zest, oil, cilantro, cumin, and cinnamon in a bowl, and mix well. Season to taste with salt; set aside.

To prepare the oysters, shuck them and refrigerate the meat until you are ready to cook them. Reserve and wash the bottom half of each shell; set aside.

Combine the eggs and water in a bowl, and mix well. In another bowl, combine the flour and cornmeal, mix well, add the salt and pepper, and mix well again. Dip each oyster in the egg mixture, then dredge in the flour mixture, and place on a plate.

Heat the oil in a large sauté pan over high heat until smoking hot. Add as many oysters as will fit in the pan without overcrowding and brown well, about 2 minutes per side. Drain on paper towels. Continue pan-frying the remaining oysters.

To serve, place an oyster in each of the reserved shells. Set the shells on a bed of rock salt on a serving platter or tray. Top the oysters with some of the relish, garnish with cilantro sprigs, and serve immediately.

Cornmeal Blini with Smoked Salmon and Saffron Crème Fraîche

Serves 6

SAFFRON CRÈME FRAÎCHE
³/₄ cup crème fraîche (page 181)
2 teaspoons chopped fresh dill
1 clove garlic, minced
Finely grated zest of 1 lemon
1 large pinch of saffron

BLINI
1 ¹/₂ cups milk
1 teaspoon active dry yeast
1 tablespoon sugar
1 ¹/₄ cups all-purpose flour
2 large eggs, separated
3 tablespoons unsalted butter, at room temperature
¹/₄ cup finely ground cornmeal
¹/₂ teaspoon salt
2 teaspoons vegetable oil

12 ounces hot-smoked salmon

To prepare the saffron crème fraîche, combine all the ingredients in a bowl and mix well. Cover and refrigerate until you are ready to serve.

To prepare the blini batter, heat the milk in a saucepan over medium heat until it reaches 100° to 110°F, and you can feel the heat with your fingertip. Pour the milk into a large bowl, add the yeast, sugar, and ¹/₂ cup of the flour, and mix well. Cover with plastic wrap, and let the dough rise in a warm place until doubled in bulk, about 1 ¹/₂ hours. Add the egg yolks, butter, cornmeal, salt, and the remaining ³/₄ cup flour, and mix well. Again cover and let rise until doubled in bulk, about 1 ¹/₂ hours. When the dough has risen, place the egg whites into the clean bowl of a standing mixer fitted with the whip attachment, and whip until they hold soft peaks. Fold the whites into the batter.

To cook the blini, heat a large nonstick sauté pan or a griddle over medium heat until warm (if it is too hot, the delicate batter might burn). Brush the pan with some of the oil. Using a 2-ounce ladle, form as many pancakes as will fit without overcrowding the pan, and cook until golden brown, 2 to 3 minutes per side. Keep warm. Repeat until all the batter is used, brushing the pan with more oil as needed.

To serve, place two blini on each plate, and divide the smoked salmon among the blini. Top with a dollop of the crème fraîche. Serve warm or at room temperature.

Chilled Roasted Red Pepper Soup with Avocado-Chile Salsa

Serves 6

SOUP

1 tablespoon extra virgin olive oil

1 small onion, minced

3 cloves garlic, chopped

2 teaspoons ground cumin

1 cup Marsala

6 red bell peppers, roasted, peeled, seeded (see page 187), and diced

2 $1/2$ cups rich chicken stock (page 184) or vegetable stock (page 186), or more as needed

1 tablespoon chopped fresh cilantro

Salt and freshly ground black pepper

AVOCADO-CHILE SALSA

$1/2$ onion, minced

2 cloves garlic, minced

2 Anaheim chiles, roasted, peeled, seeded (see page 187), and chopped

1 dried ancho chile, roasted and pulverized (see page 187)

2 avocados, cut into small dice

Juice of 2 limes

Salt and freshly ground black pepper

$1/2$ cup crème fraîche (page 181) or sour cream, for garnish

Cilantro sprigs, for garnish

To make the soup, heat the oil in a large saucepan over high heat until very hot. Add the onion and garlic, and sauté for about 2 minutes. Add the cumin and sauté for 2 minutes longer. Add the Marsala and reduce until about $1/2$ cup remains, about 4 minutes. Add the peppers and stock, decrease the heat to medium, and simmer for about 20 minutes. Add the cilantro and season to taste with salt and pepper.

Carefully purée the soup in a blender. Transfer the soup to a large bowl, cover, and refrigerate until well chilled, about 2 hours. (If the soup is too thick after chilling, thin it down with a bit more stock.)

Meanwhile, to prepare the salsa, combine the onion, garlic, chiles, and avocados in a bowl, and mix well. Add the lime juice, mix well, and season to taste with salt and pepper. Cover and refrigerate until you are ready to serve.

To serve, ladle the soup into bowls, and garnish with the salsa, crème fraîche, and a cilantro sprig.

Black-Eyed Pea and Wild Mushroom Soup with Roasted Garlic-Herb Topping

Serves 6

SOUP

2 tablespoon extra virgin olive oil

$^1/_2$ onion, minced

2 cloves garlic, chopped

4 cups sliced wild mushrooms, such as chanterelle and porcini

1 cup Madeira

$^1/_2$ cup brandy

3 cups mushroom stock (page 185) or chicken stock (page 184)

1 $^1/_2$ cups dried black-eyed peas, cooked until al dente (page 187)

Salt and freshly ground black pepper

ROASTED GARLIC-HERB TOPPING

1 head garlic, roasted (see page 187)

2 teaspoons chopped fresh basil

2 teaspoons chopped fresh marjoram

2 teaspoons chopped fresh thyme

1 teaspoon chopped fresh rosemary

$^1/_2$ cup finely shredded good-quality Parmesan cheese

2 tablespoons extra virgin olive oil

To prepare the soup, heat the oil in a large stockpot over high heat. Add the onion and garlic, and sauté for 2 minutes. Add the mushrooms and sauté until they begin to soften, about 3 minutes. Remove the pot from the heat, add the Madeira and brandy, and then set the pot back on the burner and reduce over high heat until about $^1/_4$ cup of liquid remains. Add the stock, decrease the heat to medium, and cook for about 15 minutes. Add the beans and cook just until tender, about 10 minutes longer. Season to taste with salt and pepper.

While the soup is cooking, prepare the topping. Combine the roasted garlic, basil, marjoram, thyme, rosemary, and Parmesan cheese in a bowl, and mix well. Add the oil and mix well.

To serve, ladle the soup into bowls and sprinkle with some of the topping. Serve warm.

Fresh Pea Soup Infused with Mint

Serves 6

2 teaspoons extra virgin olive oil

2 cloves garlic, chopped

1 small onion, diced

1 cup dry sherry

3 cups freshly shelled peas

1 celeriac, peeled and diced

3 cups vegetable stock (page 186) or chicken stock
(page 184)

$^1/_4$ cup mint leaves

1 teaspoon chopped fresh tarragon

Salt and freshly ground black pepper

$^1/_2$ cup sour cream, for garnish

Mint sprigs, for garnish

Heat the oil in a large saucepan or stockpot over high heat until very hot. Add the garlic and onion, and sauté for about 2 minutes. Add the sherry and reduce until about $^1/_4$ cup of liquid remains, about 5 minutes. Add the peas, celeriac, stock, mint, and tarragon, and cook until the celeriac is tender, about 15 minutes. Transfer the soup to a blender and purée until smooth, then pour it back into the pan. Season to taste with salt and pepper. Serve hot, topped with sour cream and garnished with mint sprigs.

Tomato Soup with Wild Rice

Serves 6

1 tablespoon extra virgin olive oil

3 cloves garlic, chopped

1 large onion, cut into small dice

1 cup red wine

1 cup Madeira

3 pounds very ripe tomatoes, diced

1 tablespoon tomato paste

4 cups vegetable stock (page 186) or chicken stock
(page 184)

2 teaspoons chopped fresh flat-leaf parsley

2 teaspoons chopped fresh marjoram

Salt and freshly ground black pepper

2 cups cooked wild rice (page 183)

Flat-leaf parsley sprigs, for garnish

Heat the oil in a large stockpot over high heat until very hot. Add the garlic and onion, and sauté for 2 to 3 minutes. Add the red wine and Madeira and reduce until about $^1/_2$ cup of liquid remains, about 5 minutes. Add the tomatoes, tomato paste, stock, chopped parsley, and marjoram, and simmer over medium heat for about 1 hour.

Transfer the mixture to a blender and purée. Then strain the soup back into the stockpot. Season to taste with salt and pepper. Add the rice and cook over medium heat until hot. Serve hot, garnished with parsley sprigs.

Savannah's Clam Chowder

Serves 8

1 cup dry white wine
2 teaspoons unsalted butter
3 pounds fresh clams, rinsed
8 slices pepper bacon or bacon, diced
1 onion, diced
2 cloves garlic, chopped
3 stalks celery, diced
2 tablespoons all-purpose flour
1 cup dry sherry
3 cups fish stock (page 184)
1 tablespoon chopped fresh thyme
2 teaspoons chopped fresh basil
3 Yukon Gold potatoes, peeled and diced
1 cup half-and-half
6 dashes of Tabasco sauce
4 dashes of Worcestershire sauce
Salt and freshly ground black pepper
Thyme sprigs, for garnish

Combine the wine and butter in a large stockpot over high heat and bring to a boil. Add the clams, cover, and cook for about 3 minutes. Stir well and continue cooking until the clams open, about 4 minutes longer (discard any that don't open). Remove the pan from the heat, strain off and reserve the cooking liquid, and let the clams cool for a few minutes. When the clams are cool enough to handle, remove the meat from the shells; set aside.

Heat the stockpot over medium heat until hot. Add the bacon and cook until crispy, about 4 minutes. Transfer the bacon to a paper towel to drain, reserving the drippings in the pot. Add the onion, garlic, and celery to the pot, and sauté for about 3 minutes. Sprinkle the flour over the vegetables and sauté for 2 minutes longer. Slowly whisk in the sherry. Add the fish stock, reserved cooking liquid from the clams, thyme, basil, and potatoes. Simmer until the potatoes are tender, 10 to 15 minutes. Add the half-and-half, Tabasco, and Worcestershire sauce, and bring to a boil. Season to taste with salt and pepper. Add the reserved clams and bacon, and cook over medium heat just until the clams are warm, 3 to 4 minutes. Serve warm, garnished with thyme.

Ginger- and Lemon-Scented Chicken Broth with Grilled Prawns

Serves 6

CHICKEN BROTH
1/2 onion, diced
1 tablespoon peeled, grated fresh ginger
2 cloves garlic, chopped
1 stalk fresh lemongrass, chopped
1 tablespoon chopped fresh basil
1 cup dry sherry
5 cups rich chicken stock (page 184)
Salt and freshly ground black pepper

GRILLED PRAWNS
18 extra-large prawns, peeled and deveined, tails intact
6 stalks fresh lemongrass (optional)
1 clove garlic, minced
1 tablespoon five-spice powder
2 tablespoons vegetable oil
Salt and freshly ground black pepper
1 lemon, cut into 6 slices

To make the broth, combine the onion, ginger, garlic, lemongrass, basil, and sherry in a large saucepan over high heat, and reduce until about 1/4 cup of liquid remains, 4 to 5 minutes. Add the chicken stock, decrease the heat to medium, and simmer for about 20 minutes. Strain the stock through a fine-mesh sieve, and season to taste with salt and pepper. Keep warm or refrigerate until you are ready to use it.

To prepare the prawns, oil the grill and prepare a hot fire. If you are using a gas grill, preheat on high. If you are using a charcoal grill, let the coals burn until they are covered with gray ash. The fire is hot when you can hold your hand over the grill for no longer than 2 seconds.

Skewer three prawns on each stalk of lemongrass (or on wooden skewers soaked in water for 10 minutes). Place the skewers in a shallow dish and toss with the garlic, five-spice, and 1 tablespoon of the vegetable oil. Season with salt and black pepper. In a small bowl, toss the lemon slices with the remaining 1 tablespoon vegetable oil.

Place the skewers and lemon slices on the hot grill. Grill the prawns just until they turn pink, about 2 minutes per side, and grill the lemon slices just until they have grill marks, about 1 minute per side.

To serve, ladle the broth into bowls. Float a lemon slice in each bowl, and set a skewer of prawns across the top of the bowl. Serve warm.

Menus: Entrées with Side Dishes

Menu 1:

Grilled Portobello Mushrooms with Roasted Onions and Pears

We let this multilayered entrée speak for itself when serving it at the table. With the meaty, earthy grilled mushrooms infused with the lively marinade, and the meltingly tender onions and pears, we don't want a side dish to distract the palate from this rustic (but by no means simple) dish. Instead, we choose to begin the meal with one special appetizer, such as Black Pepper–Encrusted Scallops with Mint Yogurt Sauce (page 14), served as a first course. This makes choosing the wine more of an adventure, since each course calls for its own varietal. To begin, an Alsatian Pinot Blanc will hold its own when paired with the boldly peppered scallops. The second course transitions nicely with the help of an assertive, juicy Pinot Noir.

Grilled Portobello Mushrooms with Roasted Onions and Pears

Serves 6

MARINADE
1 cup Pinot Gris
$^{1}/_{4}$ cup extra virgin olive oil
3 tablespoons sherry vinegar
2 tablespoons apple juice concentrate
2 tablespoons walnut oil
1 tablespoon chopped fresh thyme
2 cloves garlic, chopped

6 large portobello mushrooms, stems removed

2 tablespoons extra virgin olive oil
3 large onions, cut into 6 wedges
6 pears, peeled, cored, and quartered
Salt and freshly ground black pepper
Thyme sprigs, for garnish

To prepare the marinade, whisk together the wine, olive oil, vinegar, apple juice concentrate, walnut oil, thyme, and garlic in a bowl. Place the mushrooms in a large baking dish, pour the marinade over the mushrooms, and let sit at room temperature for 1 hour to marinate.

Preheat the oven to 425°F.

Meanwhile, prepare the onions and pears. Place a roasting pan in the oven to preheat for about 10 minutes. Add the olive oil and onions to the hot pan, toss to coat, and roast, without stirring, until brown, about 20 minutes. Add the pears, toss well, and cook until tender, about 15 minutes.

While the pears are cooking, oil the grill and prepare a hot fire. If you are using a gas grill, preheat on high. If you are using a charcoal grill, let the coals burn down until they are covered with gray ash. The fire is hot when you can hold your hand over the grill for no longer than 5 seconds.

When the pears are tender, remove the pan from the oven and set it over two burners. Add the mushroom marinade, reserving the mushrooms, and cook until reduced by about half, about 5 minutes. Remove the pan from the heat, and season the mixture to taste with salt and pepper. Keep warm.

To grill the mushrooms, place them on the hot grill and grill until tender, 6 to 7 minutes per side.

To serve, arrange the onions and pears on a serving platter, top with the grilled mushrooms, drizzle with the mushroom marinade, and garnish with thyme sprigs. Serve warm.

Cook One:

Make the marinade and marinate the mushrooms.

Oil and light the grill.

Grill the mushrooms.

Plate and garnish the dish.

Cook Two:

Prep the onions and the pears.

Preheat a roasting pan and roast the onions and pears.

Remove the pears and onions from the oven and finish the sauce.

Open and pour the wine.

Sweet Peppers Stuffed with Masa Harina, Caramelized Onions, and Manchego Cheese

Menu 2:

Sweet Peppers Stuffed with Masa Harina, Caramelized Onions, and Manchego Cheese

Romaine Tossed with Creamy Buttermilk Dressing

We came up with this entrée one evening when a craving for tamales hit. We had just about everything necessary in our pantry—except for that essential tamale ingredient, corn husks. Not to be deterred, we searched the refrigerator for a substitute and found sweet bell peppers. Unlike traditional tamales that have to be unwrapped before eaten, we were intrigued by the idea of putting the filling in peppers and then being able to enjoy the whole thing. Our experiment was a visual and culinary success: bright red towers of peppers with crispy, golden brown filling. We proudly toasted our accomplishment with fresh mango margaritas.

Serves 6

2 tablespoons extra virgin olive oil
2 small onions, diced
3 cloves garlic, minced
1 cup dry sherry
1 cup grated manchego cheese
3 1/2 cups masa harina
2 1/4 cups chicken stock (page 184)
1 1/4 cups unsalted butter, softened
2 tablespoons ground cumin
1 tablespoon kosher salt
1 1/2 teaspoons baking powder
1 teaspoon crushed red pepper flakes
1 tablespoon smoked paprika
6 whole red bell peppers, tops removed, and seeded
Cilantro sprigs, for garnish

Preheat the oven to 350°F.

To prepare the filling, heat the oil in a large sauté pan until very hot. Add the onions and cook, without stirring, for 6 to 8 minutes. Toss and continue to cook until well caramelized and golden brown, about 20 minutes total cooking time. Add the garlic and cook for about 1 minute, then add the sherry and cook until the mixture is almost dry, about 4 minutes. Remove from the heat and let cool. When cool, fold in the cheese and set aside.

In a medium bowl, combine the masa harina and stock and whisk until smooth, adding hot water if the mixture is too thick.

In the bowl of a mixer, combine the butter, cumin, salt, baking powder, red pepper flakes, and 2 teaspoons of the paprika. Whip on high speed until fluffy. Lower the speed and add the reconstituted masa, a tablespoon or so at a time, and beat until well blended. Next, add the cooled onion mixture and mix well. Distribute the filling among the peppers. Place the stuffed peppers in a 9 by 13-inch baking dish. Bake the peppers for about 30 minutes, until the filling is hot.

To serve, place each pepper on a plate, garnish with cilantro sprigs, and dust the edge of the plates with the remaining 1 teaspoon smoked paprika. Serve hot.

Cook One:

Caramelize the onions and let cool.

Prep the peppers.

Make the salad dressing.

Toss and plate the salad.

Cook Two:

Make the filling for the peppers.

Stuff and bake the peppers.

Clean the lettuce and prep the onion and nuts for the salad.

Plate the peppers.

Romaine Tossed with Creamy Buttermilk Dressing

Serves 6

CREAMY BUTTERMILK DRESSING
2 tablespoons cider vinegar
2 cloves garlic, chopped
2 teaspoons Dijon mustard
1 large egg yolk
$^2/_3$ cup extra virgin olive oil
$^1/_3$ cup buttermilk
1 tablespoon chopped fresh basil
Salt and freshly ground black pepper

2 heads Romaine lettuce, rinsed well, spun dry, and torn into bite-sized pieces
1 small red onion, julienned
$^1/_2$ cup chopped toasted pecans (see page 188)

To prepare the dressing, combine the vinegar, garlic, mustard, and egg yolk in a blender and blend until smooth. Add the oil and blend until smooth. Add the buttermilk and basil, and blend until smooth. Season to taste with salt and pepper.

To prepare the salad, combine the lettuce and onion in a large salad bowl. Toss well. Add enough of the dressing to coat the greens, and toss well. Garnish with toasted pecans, and serve immediately.

French-Style Pizza Royale

Menu 3:

French-Style Pizza Royale

Butter Lettuce Salad with Champagne Vinaigrette

It's hard to believe we came away from a trip to France inspired to make pizza. As only the French would, they topped this pizza with a rich garlic cream sauce, bacon, caramelized sweet onions, and cheese, of course. The key element of the recipe is a pizza or baking stone, an extremely useful baking tool that provides a crust superior to one baked on a sheet pan, not only for pizza but also other breads and rolls. Most home ovens only have room for one pizza stone, which means cooking just one pizza at a time. We simply have the table set and the salad ready, so when that first hot and crispy pizza comes out of the oven everyone can enjoy it while the second one bakes. With the creamy sauce and the sweet onions, we like to serve a bright white wine from France's Loire Valley, a blend of Chenin Blanc, Sauvignon Blanc, and Chardonnay.

French-Style Pizza Royale

Serves 6; makes two 12-inch pizzas

PIZZA DOUGH
1 tablespoon active dry yeast
Pinch of sugar
1 $^1/_4$ cups warm water (105° to 115°F)
2 tablespoons extra virgin olive oil
2 cloves garlic, chopped
3 cups all-purpose flour
1 teaspoon salt

GARLIC CREAM SAUCE
$^1/_2$ cup dry white wine
1 shallot, chopped
4 cloves garlic, chopped
1 $^1/_2$ cups heavy whipping cream
Salt and freshly ground black pepper

TOPPINGS
5 slices bacon, diced
1 tablespoon extra virgin olive oil
2 sweet onions, cubed
1 cup grated fontina cheese

To prepare the dough, combine the yeast, sugar, and water in the bowl of a mixer fitted with the paddle attachment, and mix on low speed until the yeast has dissolved. Let stand until the mixture is creamy and foamy, about 10 minutes. Add the oil, garlic, and 1 cup of the flour, and mix to form a soft dough. Add the remaining 2 cups flour, about $^1/_2$ cup at a time, mixing well after each addition. Add the salt and mix on low speed until the dough is smooth and elastic, about 5 minutes. Transfer the dough to a well-floured board and knead to form a smooth ball, about 5 minutes. Oil a large bowl with olive oil, place the dough in the bowl, and cover with a clean towel or plastic wrap. Let rise in a warm place until doubled in volume, about 1 $^1/_2$ hours.

Meanwhile, to prepare the cream sauce, combine the wine, shallot, and garlic in a saucepan over high heat and reduce until about $1/4$ cup remains, about 3 minutes. Add the cream and cook over medium heat until the sauce is thick enough to coat the back of a spoon, 5 to 6 minutes. Let the sauce cool to room temperature until you are ready to assemble the pizza.

To prepare the toppings, heat a large sauté pan over medium heat until hot. Add the bacon and cook until very crispy, about 4 minutes. Transfer the bacon to a paper towel to drain, reserving the drippings in the pan. Add the olive oil and onions to the pan, and cook over medium heat, without stirring, until the onions start to brown, about 5 minutes. Toss and cook, again without stirring, until brown, about 5 minutes. Toss and continue cooking until the onions are caramelized and golden brown, 15 to 20 minutes total cooking time. (One word of caution: As the onions brown they will begin to cook faster, so keep a close eye on them as they cook.) Let the onions cool to room temperature while the dough finishes rising.

To assemble the pizza, set a pizza stone in the oven, and preheat the oven to 425°F. Cut the dough in half. On a well-floured board, roll one of the pieces of dough into a thin 12-inch circle. Place the dough on a well-floured pizza peel. Gently spread half of the cooled cream sauce over the dough, then top with half of the caramelized onions and bacon. Sprinkle with half of the cheese. Carefully slide the pizza onto the hot pizza stone in the oven, and bake for about 10 minutes, until the crust is golden brown.

Cut the pizza into 6 slices and serve warm. Assemble and bake the second pizza while you enjoy the first one.

Butter Lettuce Salad with Champagne Vinaigrette

Serves 6

CHAMPAGNE VINAIGRETTE
2 tablespoons champagne vinegar or other white wine vinegar
1 clove garlic, minced
1 small shallot, minced
$1/3$ cup extra virgin olive oil
Sea salt and freshly ground black pepper

3 heads butter lettuce, rinsed well, spun dry, and quartered
6 radishes, thinly sliced

6 thin slices red onion, for garnish

To prepare the dressing, whisk together the vinegar, garlic, and shallot in a small bowl. While whisking, slowly add the oil and whisk until smooth. Season to taste with salt and pepper. Set aside.

To serve, place two lettuce quarters on each plate and top with the radish slices. Garnish each salad with an onion ring. Drizzle with the dressing and serve immediately, or serve the dressing on the side at the table.

Cook One:

Make the pizza dough and let rise.
Make the vinaigrette for the salad.
Clean the lettuce and prep the garnishes for the salad.
Plate the salad and drizzle with the dressing.

Cook Two:

Make the garlic cream sauce.
Cook the toppings for the pizza.
Assemble and bake the pizzas.
Slice the pizzas.

Polenta Timbales with Tomatoes and Artichokes

Menu 4:

Polenta Timbales with Tomatoes and Artichokes

Grilled Endive Salad with Blue Cheese

Hosting a dinner party for vegetarians and non-vegetarians alike can be a challenge. The key to making your guests happy without having to prepare two separate meals is a versatile dish like these timbales. For the vegetarians in the group, serve the beautifully layered polenta as is for a fantastic entrée. And for the meat-eaters, skewer and grill shrimp or skirt steak and serve on top of the timbales. The salad combines an interesting blend of textures and flavors: raddichio, a bitter endive, really mellows when it is marinated and grilled, while the crumbles of blue cheese add a creamy note to play off the tang of the dressing. The salad can be served warm or at room temperature, making the whole dinner even easier for you and your cooking partner to pull together. A Côtes-du-Rhône, with its characteristic blend of many grape varietals, offers a nice complexity that makes it the natural choice for this menu.

Polenta Timbales with Tomatoes and Artichokes

Serves 6

1 tablespoon extra virgin olive oil
6 plum tomatoes, halved and seeded
3 cloves garlic, minced
6 artichoke bottoms, quartered
2 tablespoons good-quality balsamic vinegar (aged at least 5 years)
Salt and freshly ground black pepper
3 cups vegetable stock (page 186)
1 1/2 cups finely ground cornmeal
2 teaspoons cayenne sauce
3 dashes of Worcestershire sauce
1 cup grated fontina cheese
Flat-leaf parsley sprigs, for garnish

Preheat the oven to 425°F. Grease six 8-ounce ramekins; set aside.

Heat the oil in a large, ovenproof sauté pan until hot. Add the tomatoes and one-third of the garlic, set the pan in the oven, and roast the tomatoes for 8 to 10 minutes, until they start to soften. Remove the pan from the oven, add the artichoke bottoms and vinegar, and mix well. Season to taste with salt and pepper. Divide the mixture among the prepared ramekins; set aside.

To prepare the polenta, combine the stock and the remaining minced garlic in a large saucepan over high heat and bring to a boil. Slowly whisk in the cornmeal, lower the heat to medium, and cook, stirring constantly, until the polenta is very thick, like mud, 3 to 4 minutes. Remove the pan from the heat, add the cayenne sauce and Worcestershire sauce, and mix well. Season to taste with salt and pepper.

Immediately ladle some of the hot polenta over the tomato mixture in each ramekin, filling to the top. Refrigerate until set, about 1 hour.

To serve, preheat the broiler and grease a sheet pan. Turn the timbales out onto the sheet pan, keeping as much of the tomato mixture on top of the polenta as possible. Divide the grated fontina among the timbales. Place the pan under the broiler, and broil the timbales until the cheese is bubbling and lightly browned, about 5 minutes. Place each timbale on a plate, and garnish with parsley sprigs. Serve warm.

Cook One:

Prep the tomatoes, garlic, and artichoke bottoms.
Roast the tomato mixture.
Cut the radicchio and endives and marinate.
Oil and light the grill.
Grill the endives and radicchio and finish the salad.
Plate the salad.

Cook Two:

Grease the ramekins.
Make the polenta.
Prepare the timbales.
Preheat the broiler, remove the timbales from the ramekins, and top with cheese.
Finish the timbales under the broiler.

Grilled Endive Salad with Blue Cheese

Serves 6

3 heads radicchio, quartered
4 heads Belgian endives, halved
2 tablespoons sherry vinegar
2 cloves garlic, chopped
1 small shallot, chopped
$1/3$ cup extra virgin olive oil
Salt and freshly ground black pepper
3 ounces blue cheese, crumbled

Combine the radicchio and endives in a large metal bowl; set aside. Combine the vinegar, garlic, and shallot in a small bowl, and mix well. While whisking, slowly add the oil and whisk until smooth. Season to taste with salt and pepper. Pour the dressing over the greens and let marinate for about 30 minutes.

Meanwhile, oil the grill and prepare a very hot fire. If you are using a gas grill, preheat over the highest setting. If you are using a charcoal grill, let the coals burn until they are covered with gray ash. The fire is very hot when you can hold your hand over the grill for no longer than 2 seconds.

Drain the greens very well (too much vinaigrette could cause the grill to flare up and blacken the vegetables), reserving the vinaigrette in a large bowl. Grill the vegetables for 2 to 3 minutes per side. Let cool.

When the vegetables are cool enough to handle, coarsely chop, cutting around and discarding the cores. Place the vegetables in the bowl with the reserved marinade, toss well, and season to taste with salt and pepper. Add the crumbled blue cheese and toss. Serve warm or at room temperature.

Menu 5:

Risotto with Spinach and Manchego Cheese

Watercress and Pear Salad with Walnut Vinaigrette

Our favorite cured green olive for the risotto is the picholine, which is very mild and less salty than some olives, making it the perfect foil for the toasty flavor of the Spanish manchego cheese. For the salad, any type of pear will do—as long as it is ripe. The walnut oil really adds a lot of flavor, so don't skimp here (you can keep the remaining oil in the refrigerator for about 6 months).

Enlisting the help of a partner to make risotto, whether it's a simple cheese risotto for the family or a risotto with a bit more flourish like this one, makes perfect sense. With an extra pair of hands in the kitchen, the fear of serving a dish that requires your constant focus flies out the window. When we cook this menu, one of us focuses on the stirring so the other is free to pull together the remaining dishes. If you are having guests for dinner, have them lend a hand with the stirring of the risotto. They will be rewarded with a great dinner and perhaps a glass of wine—such as a Rioja—for their efforts.

Risotto with Spinach and Manchego Cheese

Serves 6

1 tablespoon extra virgin olive oil
3 cloves garlic, chopped
2 shallots, chopped
2 1/2 cups arborio rice
7 cups vegetable stock (page 186), kept at a simmer
1/2 cup cured green olives, such as picholine, coarsely chopped
Juice and finely grated zest of 1 lemon
2 cups baby spinach leaves, rinsed well and spun dry
3/4 cup grated manchego cheese
Salt and freshly ground black pepper

Heat the oil in a large saucepan over medium-high heat until hot. Add the garlic and shallots, and sauté for about 1 minute. Add the rice and sauté until the rice becomes opaque, 2 to 3 minutes. Add enough of the hot stock to just cover the rice, about 2 cups, and cook, stirring constantly, until the stock has been absorbed, about 4 minutes. Add another 1 cup of stock and continue cooking, stirring constantly, until the stock has been absorbed, about 4 minutes. Continue adding the stock, 1 cup at a time, and cooking until all of the stock has been absorbed and the rice is al dente, about 20 minutes total. Add the olives, lemon juice and zest, and spinach, and cook, stirring constantly, just until the spinach starts to wilt, about 1 minute. Remove the pan from the heat. Add about 1/2 cup of the cheese and stir until melted. Season to taste with salt and pepper. Serve in pasta plates or large, shallow bowls, topped with the remaining 1/4 cup cheese. Serve warm.

Watercress and Pear Salad with Walnut Vinaigrette

Serves 6

WALNUT VINAIGRETTE
2 tablespoons champagne vinegar
1 clove garlic, chopped
1 teaspoon Dijon mustard
$^1/_4$ cup extra virgin olive oil
2 tablespoons walnut oil
Salt and freshly ground black pepper

4 bunches watercress (about $^1/_4$ pound), rinsed well
    and spun dry
3 ripe pears, peeled and sliced
$^1/_2$ cup chopped toasted walnuts (see page 188)

To prepare the dressing, whisk together the vinegar, garlic, and mustard in a bowl. While whisking, slowly add the olive oil, and whisk until smooth and emulsified. Whisk in the walnut oil, and season to taste with salt and pepper.

To prepare the salad, divide the watercress among six salad plates. Arrange the pear slices over the watercress. Drizzle some of the dressing on each salad (save remaining dressing for another use), then top with the chopped walnuts. Serve immediately.

Cook One:

Clean the watercress.

Prep the ingredients for the risotto.

Make the risotto, enlisting Cook Two's help as the arm grows weary while stirring.

Plate and garnish the risotto.

Cook Two:

Make the salad dressing and toasted walnut garnish.

Prep the pears for the salad.

Dress the salad and plate.

Open and pour the wine.

Menu 6:

Pappardelle with Roasted Garlic and Truffle Oil

Arugula Tossed with Red Wine–Caper Dressing

Pasta will never wear out its welcome at our dinner table. We never find ourselves at a loss when preparing this irreplaceable mainstay that takes on any shape, cuisine, and cooking method. Here we use a wide-cut noodle that makes an ideal vehicle for mellow roasted garlic, salt-tinged aged cheese, and a superlative oil perfumed with pungent truffles. The understated sophistication of the dish wipes away any mundane notions our guests might have about such a common staple. A polished Chianti, such as a Ruffino Chianti Classico Riserva, is our final luxurious touch to the meal.

Pappardelle with Roasted Garlic and Truffle Oil

Serves 6

1 1/2 pound fresh pappardelle pasta
2 heads garlic, roasted (see page 187)
1/4 cup extra virgin olive oil
1 tablespoon chopped fresh flat-leaf parsley
Salt and freshly ground black pepper
4 ounces Asiago cheese, shaved
2 tablespoons black truffle oil

Bring a large pot of salted water to a boil. Add the pasta and cook until al dente, about 1 minute. Just before draining, ladle out about 1/4 cup of the cooking water and pour it into a large bowl. Drain the pasta and add to the large bowl; set aside.

In a small bowl, mash the roasted garlic with a fork. Add the oil and parsley, and mix well. Pour the garlic mixture over the pasta and toss well. Season to taste with salt and pepper.

To serve, divide the pasta among six plates, top each with cheese, and drizzle with the truffle oil. Serve warm.

Arugula Tossed with Red Wine–Caper Dressing

Serves 6

DRESSING
2 tablespoons red wine vinegar
1 clove garlic, chopped
1 small shallot, chopped
1 salt-packed anchovy fillet, minced
2 teaspoons chopped drained capers
$^1/_3$ cup extra virgin olive oil
Salt and black pepper

1 $^1/_2$ pounds arugula, rinsed well and spun dry
4 button mushrooms, sliced paper-thin
2 vine-ripened tomatoes, seeded (see page 188) and diced
$^1/_2$ cup toasted breadcrumbs (page 181)

To prepare the dressing, whisk together the vinegar, garlic, shallot, and anchovy in a small bowl. While whisking, slowly add the oil and whisk until smooth. Season to taste with salt and pepper. Set aside until you are ready to serve.

To prepare the salad, combine the arugula, mushrooms, and tomatoes in a large salad bowl, and toss well. Add enough of the dressing to coat the leaves, and toss well. Divide the salad among six plates, and sprinkle with the breadcrumbs. Serve immediately.

Cook One:

~~*Roast the garlic.*~~
Clean the arugula.
Prep the parsley and shave the cheese for the pasta.
Finish and plate the pasta.

Cook Two:

Make the salad dressing.
Prep the mushrooms and tomatoes for the salad.
Cook the pappardelle.
Dress, toss, and plate the greens.

Menu 7:

Potato Soufflés with Chive Crème Fraîche

Frisée Salad with Warm Fig Dressing and Shaved Parmesan Cheese

There are many ingredients we could learn to live without, but potatoes are not one of them. In this set of recipes, potatoes are the star, showcased simply with a tang of horseradish and presented with a flourish at the table. For an appetizer course, the soufflés made in smaller ramekins will give any meal a sophisticated beginning. And if you decide that you just can't live with them as a vegetarian entrée, try adding crispy bacon or prosciutto to the batter along with the egg yolks. The salad we serve with the entrée has a rich dressing with sweet flavors that make a nice contrast to the savory potatoes. Try to toss the salad just as the soufflés are coming out of the oven so the frisée does not wilt too much, but don't worry if your timing is a bit off; frisée is much sturdier than other greens, so it can handle a bit more time before serving.

Potato Soufflés with Chive Crème Fraîche

Serves 6

2 tablespoons unsalted butter, at room temperature
5 Yukon Gold potatoes, peeled and diced
1 cup half-and-half
3 cloves garlic, chopped
1 teaspoon prepared horseradish
Salt and freshly ground black pepper
4 large egg yolks
6 large egg whites

CHIVE CRÈME FRAÎCHE
1 1/4 cups crème fraîche (page 181)
2 tablespoons chopped fresh chives
Salt and freshly ground black pepper

Preheat the oven to 375°F. (You will get the best results in a convection oven.) Using 1 tablespoon of the butter, butter six 8-ounce ramekins; set aside.

To prepare the soufflés, in a large saucepan, add enough cold salted water to cover the potatoes, and bring to a boil over high heat. Lower the heat to medium and cook the potatoes until tender, about 15 minutes. Drain well. Arrange the potatoes in a single layer on a sheet pan and bake to dry them, about 5 minutes. Transfer the potatoes to a ricer and rice them into a large bowl. Add the half-and-half, garlic, remaining 1 tablespoon butter, and horseradish, and mix well. Season to taste with salt and pepper. Add the egg yolks and mix well.

In the clean bowl of mixer fitted with the whip attachment, whip the egg whites until they hold soft peaks. Gently fold the whites into the potato mixture. Divide the potato mixture among the prepared ramekins. Set the ramekins on a sheet pan. Bake for 20 to 25 minutes, until the soufflés have risen and are golden brown.

(continued)

43

(continued from page 43)

Meanwhile, to prepare the chive crème fraîche, mix together the crème fraîche and chives in a small bowl, and season to taste with salt and pepper.

To serve, place the soufflés on individual plates and serve immediately. At the table, use a butter knife to poke a hole in the center of each soufflé, and then drizzle in some of the chive crème fraîche.

Cook One:

Prep the potatoes and put on to cook.

Butter the ramekins.

Make the soufflé batter up to the point of adding the egg whites.

Fill the ramekins and place the soufflés in the oven.

Shave the cheese for the salad garnish.

Remove the soufflés from the oven and place on serving plates.

Serve the soufflés.

Cook Two:

Clean the frisée and refrigerate.

Make the salad dressing.

Make the crème fraîche for the soufflés and refrigerate.

Whip the egg whites and fold into the batter.

About 10 minutes before the soufflés are finished baking, heat the dressing.

Just as the soufflés are coming out of the oven, toss, plate, garnish, and serve the salad.

Serve the crème fraîche.

Frisée Salad with Warm Fig Dressing and Shaved Parmesan Cheese

Serves 6

2 large heads frisée, rinsed well and spun dry

FIG DRESSING

1 shallot, chopped

1 clove garlic, chopped

2 dried figs, diced

1 1/2 cups red wine

2 tablespoons good-quality balsamic vinegar (aged at least 5 years)

1/3 cup extra virgin olive oil

Salt and freshly ground black pepper

2/3 cup shaved good-quality Parmesan cheese, for garnish

Place the frisée in a large metal bowl and refrigerate until you are ready to use it.

To prepare the dressing, combine the shallot, garlic, figs, and wine in a saucepan over high heat, and cook until the figs are very soft and most of the wine has reduced, about 5 minutes. Transfer to a blender, add the vinegar and oil, and purée until smooth. Season to taste with salt and pepper. Transfer the mixture to a saucepan over medium-high heat, and bring to a boil.

To serve, toss the hot dressing with the greens. Divide the salad among 4 plates, and top with Parmesan cheese. Serve warm.

<table>
<tr><td>

Menu 8:

Sautéed Potatoes and Artichokes

Watercress Salad with Warm Taleggio Cheese

Due to the delicate nature of the watercress in the salad, we serve this menu in courses. The salad is at its optimum right when the cheese hits the greens, so we don't delay serving it. Presenting the salad first gives our guests the chance to focus solely on the peppery greens topped with a melting ripened cheese. Once the plates are cleared, we introduce the artichokes and potatoes in a lemon- and thyme-infused broth. Unlike the salad, this entrée holds nicely once finished, so it can be kept warm safely while everyone enjoys the first course. Artichokes can be a tricky match with any wine, but when combined with the potatoes and stock, their fussy nature is softened, making them eligible for a lush and unctuous wine, such as Pinot Blanc.

</td></tr>
</table>

Sautéed Potatoes and Artichokes

Serves 6

9 artichokes
1 lemon, quartered
2 tablespoons extra virgin olive oil
6 large Yukon Gold potatoes, peeled and cut into large dice
3 cloves garlic, chopped
1 1/2 cups dry vermouth
2 cups vegetable stock (page 186)
1 tablespoon chopped fresh thyme
Juice and finely grated zest of 2 lemons
2 tablespoons unsalted butter
Salt and freshly ground black pepper
1 tablespoon lemon olive oil (extra virgin olive oil pressed with lemons)
Thyme sprigs, for garnish

Clean each artichoke by removing the leaves and choke, peeling the stem, and then cutting the remaining bottom in half. Place the artichokes in a large bowl of water with a squeeze of lemon; set aside.

Heat the olive oil in a large sauté pan over high heat until smoking hot. Add the potatoes and let them cook, without stirring, until brown, about 3 minutes. Drain the artichokes, add them to the potatoes, and let them cook, without stirring, until brown, about 4 minutes. Add the garlic and sauté for 1 minute. Add the vermouth and reduce over high heat until about 1/4 cup of liquid remains, about 7 minutes. Add the vegetable stock and reduce until about 1 cup of liquid remains, about 5 minutes. Add the thyme and the lemon juice and zest, and toss well. Add the butter and season to taste with salt and pepper.

To serve, arrange the potatoes and artichokes on a serving platter, drizzle with the lemon olive oil, top with the broth, and garnish with thyme sprigs. Serve warm.

Watercress Salad with Warm Taleggio Cheese

Serves 6

2 tablespoons red wine vinegar
1 shallot, minced
1 clove garlic, minced
1 tablespoon Dijon mustard
$^1/_3$ cup extra virgin olive oil
Salt and freshly ground black pepper
3 bunches watercress (about $^1/_4$ pound), rinsed well,
    spun dry, and stems trimmed
6 ($^1/_2$-inch-thick) slices Taleggio cheese
2 teaspoons dark brown sugar
2 teaspoons chopped fresh thyme

To make the dressing, whisk together the vinegar, shallot, garlic, and mustard in a small bowl until smooth. While whisking, slowly add the olive oil and whisk until smooth. Season to taste with salt and pepper. Set aside until you are ready to serve.

To prepare the salad, preheat the broiler. Place the watercress in a bowl. Lightly grease a sheet pan and place the cheese slices on the pan. Sprinkle with the brown sugar and thyme. Add the dressing to the watercress and toss. Divide the greens among the plates. Place the cheese under the broiler and cook just until the cheese starts to soften, about 1 minute. Remove from the oven and carefully place the warm cheese on top of the salads. Serve warm.

Cook One:

Prep the artichokes.

Sauté the potatoes.

Add the artichokes to the potatoes, finish cooking, and keep warm.

Broil the cheese for the salads.

When finished with the salad course, plate and garnish the potatoes and artichokes.

Cook Two:

Make the salad dressing.

Clean the watercress.

Dress the watercress.

Plate the salads and top with the cheese.

Open and serve the wine.

47

Menu 9:

Potato-Morel Gratin
Marsala-Roasted Beets

Mushroom hunting is a popular outdoor adventure for many people here in the Pacific Northwest. Although we don't get to forage for these gems of the woods as much as we used to before we had so many responsibilities and demands on our time, we have plenty of friends who venture out into the forests and share their bounty upon their return. In gratitude, we always like to prepare a feast featuring this prized ingredient, often in incarnations of this gratin. Of course, the morels we find at the market don't offer as much romance, but they bring just as much earthy aroma to our cooking. The concentrated sweetness of roasted beets served alongside the rustic gratin create a dynamic autumn pairing, made only better by pouring a Châteauneuf-du-Pape.

Potato-Morel Gratin

Serves 6

5 Yukon Gold potatoes, peeled and thinly sliced
2 tablespoons unsalted butter
2 cloves garlic, chopped
1 shallot, diced
1 pound fresh morel mushrooms
1 teaspoon chopped fresh rosemary
1 cup red wine
2 cups vegetable stock (page 186) or chicken stock (page 184)
Salt and freshly ground black pepper
1 cup fresh breadcrumbs (page 181)
$^1/_2$ cup freshly grated Parmesan cheese
1 cup grated aged Gouda cheese

Preheat the oven to 375°F.

Arrange the potatoes in a well-greased 9 by 13-inch pan and set aside.

Heat the butter in a large sauté pan over medium-high heat until melted and bubbling. Add the garlic and shallot, sauté for about 1 minute. Add the mushrooms and rosemary, and sauté for 2 to 3 minutes longer. Add the red wine and reduce until about $^1/_4$ cup of liquid remains, about 3 or 4 minutes. Add the stock, bring to a boil, and season to taste with salt and pepper. Pour the mushroom mixture over the potatoes.

In a bowl, combine the breadcrumbs and the cheeses, and sprinkle over the mushrooms.

Bake for 40 to 50 minutes, until the potatoes are tender. Let the gratin cool for about 5 minutes before serving. Serve warm.

Marsala-Roasted Beets

Serves 6

2 tablespoons extra virgin olive oil
6 beets, peeled and diced
³/₄ cup Marsala
2 cloves garlic, chopped
2 teaspoons chopped fresh thyme
Juice of ¹/₂ lemon
Salt and freshly ground black pepper
Thyme sprigs, for garnish

Preheat the oven to 425°F.

Heat the oil in a very large, ovenproof sauté pan over high heat until smoking hot. Add the beets and toss to coat with the oil. Set the pan in the oven and roast the beets, tossing once or twice, for about 20 minutes, until tender. Remove the pan from the oven and set it over high heat. Add the Marsala and reduce over high heat until about ¹/₄ cup of liquid remains, about 5 minutes. Add the garlic, thyme, and lemon juice, and cook for about 2 minutes. Season to taste with salt and pepper. Transfer the beets to a serving dish or platter, garnish with thyme sprigs, and serve warm.

Cook One:

Prep the potatoes for the gratin.

Prep the beets for the salad.

Preheat a sauté pan and roast the beets.

Plate the beets.

Cook Two:

Arrange the potatoes in a baking dish.

Make the mushroom mixture and pour over the potatoes.

Top the gratin with the cheese and breadcrumbs, and bake.

Cut and serve the gratin.

Pumpkin-Leek Tart

Menu 10:

Pumpkin-Leek Tart

Chanterelle Mushroom Salad

We are always looking for excuses to get together with our friends, whether for dinner, lunch, brunch, or morning coffee. This tart can slide into any course in just about any menu, no matter what the time of day. With its flaky crust, mild leeks, and silky filling, it is reminiscent of a classic quiche—yet it offers a fresh twist on that versatile favorite. We really like that we can serve it for brunch one day, and then serve any leftovers for an appetizer to our unsuspecting friends that night. Depending on who is coming over, we can embellish the tart with crispy bacon, prosciutto, roasted shallots, a bit of blue cheese, or any other ingredient we know they would enjoy. The tart makes an excellent backdrop for the tangy dressing and nutty essence of the chanterelle salad. With its balanced fruit and acidity, a slightly off-dry Riesling has the same affinity for the sumptuous fare.

Pumpkin-Leek Tart

Serves 6

CRUST

1 1/3 all-purpose cups flour
1/2 teaspoon salt
1/4 cup cold unsalted butter, diced
1/4 cup vegetable shortening
6 tablespoon ice water

FILLING

2 tablespoons unsalted butter
3 leeks, white parts only, cut crosswise into 1/4-inch-thick slices
3 cloves garlic, chopped
1/3 cup dry white wine
2 cups pumpkin purée
1 cup half-and-half
3 large eggs
2 teaspoons chopped fresh thyme
2 teaspoons chopped fresh marjoram
Salt and freshly ground black pepper
1 cup grated aged Gouda cheese

Preheat the oven to 400°F (you will get the best results in a convection oven). Grease a 9-inch flan or tart pan with a removable bottom.

To prepare the crust, combine the flour, salt, butter, and shortening in a large bowl. Using your fingertips, blend until the mixture resembles a coarse meal. Add the water and mix with a fork just until the dough is moistened and comes together. Turn the dough out onto a well-floured board, form it into a disk with your hands, and wrap it in plastic wrap. Refrigerate for 30 minutes.

On a well-floured board, roll out the dough into an 11-inch circle. Fit the dough into the prepared pan. Bake just until set but not brown, about 10 minutes. Let cool completely.

Decrease the oven temperature to 350°F.

(continued)

(continued from page 50)

While the crust is cooling, prepare the filling. Heat the butter in a large sauté pan over medium-high heat until melted and bubbling. Add the leeks and garlic, and sauté over medium heat until the leeks are tender, 3 to 4 minutes. Add the wine and reduce over high heat until the mixture is almost dry. Let cool until tepid.

Combine the pumpkin, half-and-half, and eggs in a large bowl, and mix well. Add the thymé, marjoram, and the cooled leeks, mix well, and season with salt and pepper.

To assemble the tart, sprinkle the cheese over the bottom of the prepared crust. Pour the pumpkin mixture into the crust.

Bake the tart for about 40 minutes, just until the filling is set and a knife inserted in the filling comes out clean. Let the tart rest for about 10 minutes before cutting and serving.

Chanterelle Mushroom Salad

Serves 6

1/4 cup unsalted butter
2 pounds fresh chanterelle mushrooms, torn in half
3 cloves garlic, chopped
2 shallots, chopped
1 cup dry sherry
2 tablespoons sherry vinegar
1 tablespoon chopped fresh flat-leaf parsley
1/2 teaspoon freshly ground black pepper
Sea salt

Heat the butter in a large sauté pan over medium-high heat until melted and bubbling. Add the mushrooms and sauté just until they start to become tender, 3 to 4 minutes. Add the garlic and shallots, and sauté for about 1 minute. Add the sherry and reduce until about 1/4 cup of liquid remains, about 3 minutes. Remove the pan from the heat. Add the vinegar, parsley, and pepper, toss well, and season to taste with sea salt. Place in a serving bowl. Serve warm or at room temperature.

Cook One:

Make the tart crust and partially bake it.
Prep the chanterelles.
Finish the mushroom salad.
Plate the mushroom salad.

Cook Two:

Make the tart filling.
Fill and bake the tart.
Cut and plate the tart.
Open and pour the wine.

Menu 11:

Baked Acorn Squash Stuffed with Wild Rice and Pecans

Apple and Cranberry Chutney

Every time we serve this fall meal, we can't help but be delighted with how absolutely pretty it looks on the plate. This vegetarian menu encompasses all the characteristic flavors of autumn cradled in a rich, mellow, tasty vessel. If time allows, make an even larger quantity of the chutney to refrigerate and keep on hand to lend its tangy brightness to many other recipes, such as roast pork loin, vegetable stews, and even a simple sandwich. To truly mark the season, we like to pour a Pinot Noir, a quintessential flavor of Oregon that celebrates this menu like no other wine could.

Baked Acorn Squash Stuffed with Wild Rice and Pecans

Serves 6

3 large acorn squash, halved and seeds removed
1 tablespoon extra virgin olive oil
1 small onion, minced
2 cloves garlic, minced
$^1/_2$ cup apple brandy or brandy
$^1/_4$ cup good-quality apple cider
3 cups cooked long-grain white rice (page 183)
3 cups cooked wild rice (page 183)
2 large egg yolks
1 cup chopped toasted pecans (see page 188)
1 cup grated aged Gouda cheese
1 tablespoon chopped fresh sage
1 tablespoon Dijon mustard
Salt and freshly ground black pepper
Sage sprigs, for garnish

Preheat the oven to 375°F. Place the squash in a large baking dish; set aside.

Heat the oil in a large sauté pan over high heat until very hot. Add the onion and garlic, and sauté for about 2 minutes. Remove the pan from the heat, then carefully add the brandy and cider. Set the pan over high heat and reduce until the mixture is almost dry, about 3 minutes. Remove the pan from the heat and let cool completely.

Transfer the cooled mixture to a large bowl. Add the white and wild rice, egg yolks, and pecans, and mix well. Add the cheese, sage, and mustard, and mix well. Season well with salt and pepper, and mix well. Divide the stuffing among the prepared squash.

Bake until the squash is tender, about 1 hour depending on the size of the squash.

Place the squash on a serving platter, and garnish with fresh sage sprigs. Serve warm.

53

Apple and Cranberry Chutney

Serves 6

1 tablespoon extra virgin olive oil
3 Granny Smith apples, peeled and diced
2 cups fresh cranberries
1 tablespoon peeled, chopped fresh ginger
3 cloves garlic, chopped
1 cup red wine
$1/2$ cup sugar
$1/4$ cup sweet-hot chile sauce
2 teaspoons chopped fresh sage
Juice and finely grated zest of 1 orange
Salt and freshly ground black pepper

Heat the oil in a very large sauté pan over high heat until smoking hot. Add the apples and cranberries, toss to coat with the oil, and sauté until the cranberries start to split, about 3 minutes. Add the ginger and garlic, and sauté for about 1 minute. Add the wine and sugar, and cook until the mixture starts to thicken, 4 to 5 minutes. Add the chile sauce, sage, and the orange juice and zest, and cook for about 2 minutes longer. Remove the pan from the heat, and season to taste with salt and pepper.

Transfer to a serving dish, and serve warm or at room temperature.

Cook One:

Prep the squash.
Finish the stuffing.
Stuff the squash and bake.

Cook Two:

Cook both types of rice for the stuffing.
Make the chutney.
Plate and garnish the squash and chutney.

Menu 12:

Cornmeal-Encrusted Green Tomatoes and Grilled Corn Salad

Cheddar Biscuits

This menu provides a wonderful way to use green tomatoes that are left on the vine after the season ends. But if you have to wait forever for your tomatoes to ripen like we do, you can use a few green ones while you wait for the rest to finish on the vine. The corn salad is served at room temperature, which means it should be finished and cooling before the tomatoes are fried. This allows you and your cooking partner to each take on a part of the tomato preparation. While one takes on the somewhat messy step of breading the tomatoes, the other can focus on frying them to golden perfection. A light red wine with a bit of fruit like an Italian nebbiolo makes an excellent beverage for the beginning or end of summer.

Cornmeal-Encrusted Green Tomatoes and Grilled Corn Salad

Serves 6

GRILLED CORN SALAD
5 ears corn, shucked
$1/3$ cup plus 1 tablespoon extra virgin olive oil
3 cloves garlic, minced
1 red onion, julienned
2 ripe tomatoes, seeded (see page 188) and diced
2 red bell peppers, roasted, peeled, seeded (see page 187), and diced
1 jalapeño, seeded and minced
2 teaspoons chopped fresh cilantro
2 tablespoons red wine vinegar
Salt
2 teaspoons freshly ground black pepper

TOMATOES
6 green tomatoes, sliced about $1/2$ inch thick
Salt and freshly ground black pepper
2 cups finely grated Monterey Jack cheese
2 cups all-purpose flour
4 large eggs, whisked until smooth
4 cups finely ground cornmeal
$1/2$ cup extra virgin olive oil
$2/3$ cup sour cream, as accompaniment

Cilantro sprigs, for garnish

To prepare the corn salad, oil the grill and prepare a hot fire. If you are using a gas grill, preheat on high. If you are using a charcoal grill, let the coals burn until they are covered with gray ash. The fire is hot when you can hold your hand over the grill for no longer than 5 seconds.

Brush the corn with 1 tablespoon of the oil, place them on the grill, and grill, turning often so they don't burn, until brown, 5 to 7 minutes. Let cool.

(continued)

(continued from page 56)

While the corn is grilling, combine the garlic, onion, tomatoes, bell peppers, jalapeño, and cilantro in a medium bowl, and mix well. In a small bowl, whisk together the vinegar and the remaining $1/3$ cup oil, and pour it over the vegetables. When the corn is cool, cut the kernels off the cobs. Add the corn to the salad and toss well. Season to taste with salt and the pepper. Set aside until you are ready to serve. (If the salad is prepared more than 30 before serving, refrigerate it until you are ready to serve.)

To prepare the tomatoes, lay the slices out on a sheet pan and season with salt and pepper. Distribute the cheese over the tops of the slices, pressing firmly to help it adhere; set aside. Place the flour on a large plate, the eggs in a pie plate, and the cornmeal on a large plate. Carefully dredge the prepared tomato slices in the flour, dip them in the egg mixture, then dredge in the cornmeal; return to the sheet pan.

Heat the oil in a very large skillet over high heat until it reaches 350°F. Add as many tomato slices as will fit in the pan without overcrowding and cook until golden brown, 2 to 3 minutes per side. Drain on paper towels, and keep warm. Continue with the remaining slices.

To serve, place about three of the slices on each plate, and top each slice with some of the corn salad. Top with a dollop of sour cream and garnish with cilantro sprigs. Serve immediately.

Cheddar Biscuits

Makes 12

14 tablespoons cold unsalted butter
3 cups all-purpose flour
2 cups grated sharp Cheddar cheese
1 tablespoon plus 1 teaspoon baking powder
1 $1/2$ teaspoons salt
1 teaspoon sugar
1 $1/2$ cups buttermilk

Preheat the oven to 375°F. (You will get the best results in a convection oven.) Grease a sheet pan well.

Dice 12 tablespoons ($3/4$ cup) butter. Melt the remaining 2 tablespoons.

Combine the flour, cheese, diced cold butter, baking powder, salt, and sugar in a bowl. Using your fingertips, mix until the mixture resembles a coarse meal. Add the buttermilk and mix with a fork just until the dough barely comes together. Turn the dough out onto a well-floured board and use your hands to form it into a rectangle about $1/2$ inch thick. With a knife, cut the dough into twelve equal-size biscuits. Place the biscuits on the prepared pan.

Bake the biscuits for 12 to 15 minutes, until golden brown. Remove the biscuits from the oven, and brush with the melted butter. Serve warm.

Cook One:

Oil and light the grill.

Grill the corn.

Prep the salad ingredients.

Finish preparing the salad.

Set up the breading station with bowls of flour, egg, and cornmeal.

Bread the tomatoes.

Fry the tomatoes.

Plate and garnish the tomatoes.

Cook Two:

Roast the peppers.

Cut the cooled corn.

Slice the tomatoes.

Season the tomatoes and top with cheese.

Prepare and bake the biscuits.

Help Cook One fry the tomatoes.

Brush the warm biscuits with butter, and plate.

Open and serve the wine.

Menu 13:

Seared Halibut with Quick Tomato and Cured Olive Sauce

Spaghetti with Anchovy Butter

We developed this set of recipes for a class we taught at our cooking school on everyday cooking, called "Cooking from the Pantry." We realized that what makes it easy for us to cook at home is not that we are professional chefs, but rather that we keep a good supply of basic, yet quality ingredients that inspire that creative spark. In the class, we showed our students how to put together a pantry that will yield many weeknight dinners in 20 minutes or less. Far better and almost as quick as a store-bought sauce, this tomato sauce can be made in a double batch to be frozen for those really busy days. Don't be frightened by the anchovies—we usually don't eat them whole, but when finely chopped, they add a pleasantly salty element to the dish. You can plate this individually or on a serving platter, but either way we like to put the pasta down first, then layer it with some of the sauce and the golden brown fish. Serve the remaining sauce on the side.

Seared Halibut with Quick Tomato and Cured Olive Sauce

Serves 6

QUICK TOMATO AND CURED OLIVE SAUCE
2 cloves garlic, chopped
$1/2$ onion, minced
1 cup red wine
2 cups oil-cured tomatoes or chopped ripe
  fresh tomatoes
1 tablespoon chopped fresh basil
1 teaspoon chopped fresh thyme
1 teaspoon chopped fresh oregano
1 cup chicken stock (page 184) or fish stock (page 184)
$1/2$ cup chopped cured black olives
Salt and freshly ground black pepper

$1/2$ cup all-purpose flour
$1/4$ cup finely ground cornmeal
1 tablespoon smoked paprika
6 (6-ounce) halibut fillets
Salt and freshly ground black pepper
1 tablespoon extra virgin olive oil

Oregano sprigs, for garnish

Preheat the oven to 425°F.

To prepare the tomato sauce, combine the garlic, onion, and wine in a saucepan over high heat, and reduce until about $1/4$ cup of wine remains, about 5 minutes. Add the tomatoes, basil, thyme, oregano, and stock, and bring to a boil. Decrease the heat and simmer for about 10 minutes. Add the olives and season to taste with salt and pepper. Keep warm until you are ready to serve.

To prepare the halibut, combine the flour, cornmeal, and paprika in a small bowl, and mix well. Season the fillets with salt and pepper. Heat the olive oil in a large, ovenproof sauté pan over high heat until very hot. Dredge the seasoned fillets in the flour mixture, place them in the hot pan, and sear well, 2 to 3 minutes per side. Place the pan in the oven and roast the halibut until just cooked through, about 5 minutes, depending on the thickness of the fillets. Transfer the halibut to a serving platter.

To serve, pour some of the sauce over the halibut. Garnish with oregano sprigs. Serve warm, with the remaining sauce on the side.

Cook One:

Start the reduction for the tomato sauce.
Finish the tomato sauce, and keep warm.
Cook the spaghetti.
Toss the pasta with the anchovy butter.

Cook Two:

Make the anchovy butter.
Make the seasoned flour for the halibut.
Sear the halibut and finish in the oven.
Plate and garnish the pasta, sauce, and halibut.

Spaghetti with Anchovy Butter

Serves 6

3 oil- or salt-packed anchovy fillets
3 cloves garlic
2 tablespoons chopped fresh flat-leaf parsley
2 tablespoons chopped fresh basil
Juice and finely grated zest of 2 lemons
1/2 cup unsalted butter, at room temperature
Salt and freshly ground black pepper
1 pound spaghetti
Flat-leaf parsley or basil sprigs, for garnish

Chop the anchovies and garlic together until minced, and place in a bowl. Add the parsley, basil, and the lemon juice and zest, and mix well. Add the butter and mix until smooth. Season to taste with salt and pepper. Set aside at room temperature if you will be using it right away, or refrigerate it until you are ready to use it.

Bring a large pot of salted water to a boil. Add the spaghetti and cook until al dente, about 7 minutes. Drain well and return to the pot. Add the anchovy butter and toss well to coat. (If the butter is cold, set the pan over low heat until the butter is melted.)

Transfer the pasta to a serving bowl or a platter, and garnish with fresh parsley. Serve warm.

Menu 14:

Grilled Salmon Fillets
with Basil Compound Butter

Roasted Tomato Salad

Basmati Rice with Cumin

When we make this compound butter, we always prepare a double batch to have on hand to toss with pasta, sautéed vegetables, and baked potatoes. Try different fresh herbs and spices—and, as always, take advantage of the best seafood the season has to offer. With ripe tomatoes and fresh basil, this epitome of a great summer salad is also wonderful as a topping for grilled fish or as a finish to pasta and risotto. You can vary it by adding other fresh herbs or even heirloom tomatoes from your garden or farmers' market. This method for cooking fragrant basmati rice is so foolproof that you will be encouraged to experiment with different flavors. We like to toast this beautiful menu with a Chianti Riserva.

Grilled Salmon Fillets
with Basil Compound Butter

Serves 6

BASIL COMPOUND BUTTER
1 cup fresh basil leaves
1 head garlic, roasted (see page 187)
Juice and finely grated zest of 1 lemon
$^3/_4$ cup cold unsalted butter, diced
5 dashes of Tabasco sauce
Salt and freshly ground black pepper

6 (6-ounce) skinless salmon fillets
Salt and freshly ground black pepper
1 tablespoon extra virgin olive oil

Basil sprigs, for garnish
$^1/_2$ fresh lemon, sliced, for garnish

To prepare the compound butter, purée the basil and garlic in a food processor. Add the lemon juice and zest, butter, and Tabasco. Process until smooth; season to taste with salt and pepper. Place the compound butter in a piping bag fitted with a medium star tip and pipe six 1-inch rosettes onto a parchment paper–lined sheet pan. Refrigerate until ready to use.

To prepare the salmon, oil the grill and prepare a hot fire. If you are using a gas grill, preheat over high heat. If you are using a charcoal grill, let the coals burn until they are covered with gray ash. The fire is hot when you can hold your hand over the grill for no longer than 5 seconds. Season the fillets with salt and black pepper, and brush them with the oil.

Arrange the fillets on the hot grill and grill, without turning, for about 2 minutes, then give them a quarter of a turn and let them cook for 2 minutes longer. Turn the fillets over and repeat the cooking process. Remove the salmon from the grill and place a compound butter rosette on each fillet.

Serve hot, garnished with lemon slices and basil sprigs.

Roasted Tomato Salad

Serves 6

$^1/_4$ cup extra virgin olive oil

12 very ripe plum tomatoes, halved

4 cloves garlic

4 shallots, halved

1 tablespoon chopped fresh basil

1 tablespoon sherry vinegar

Sea salt and freshly ground black pepper

Preheat the oven to 400°F.

Heat 2 tablespoons of the oil in a very large, ovenproof sauté pan over high heat until smoking hot. Add the tomatoes and toss to coat with the oil. Add the garlic and shallots, set the pan in the oven, and roast until the shallots and garlic are fork-tender, about 40 minutes.

Remove the pan from the oven, add the basil and vinegar, and toss well. Season to taste with salt and pepper. Serve warm or at room temperature.

Cook One:

Start preparing the roasted tomato salad.

Oil and light the grill.

Finish preparing the tomato salad.

Grill the salmon.

Plate the salmon, top with compound butter, and garnish.

Open and pour the wine.

Cook Two:

Roast the garlic for the compound butter.

Make the compound butter and refrigerate.

Make the rice.

Plate the tomato salad and the rice.

Basmati Rice with Cumin

Serves 6

1 $^1/_2$ cups basmati rice

1 tablespoon vegetable oil

2 cloves garlic, chopped

$^1/_2$ small onion, minced

2 tablespoons ground cumin

3 cups chicken stock (page 184) or vegetable stock (page 186)

Salt and freshly ground black pepper

Preheat the oven to 350°F. Rinse the rice in a sieve under cold running water until the water runs clear; drain well.

Heat the oil in a large saucepan over high heat until hot, add the garlic and onion, and sauté for about 1 minute. Add the cumin and sauté for about 1 minute longer. Add the rice and sauté until well-coated with the oil, about 1 minute. Add the stock, and season to taste with salt and pepper. Bring to a boil. Cover the pan with the lid or foil, place it in the oven, and bake the rice for 10 minutes. Stir well, cover, and bake until tender, about 15 minutes longer.

Fluff with a fork, and adjust the seasonings if needed. Serve warm.

Menu 15:

Oven-Baked Salmon with Picholine Olive Sauce

Orzo with Fried Shallots

Oven-Roasted Garlic Shoots with Lemon Olive Oil

As Oregonians, we are truly spoiled with the abundance of fresh salmon available practically year-round. With such an amazing resource, we really like to show it off. No matter how you cut it, salmon is always tasty. This menu features an entire side of salmon to make a big impact at the table. The side dishes include products that not everyone may be familiar with, but they aren't as exotic as they sound. Orzo is nothing more than a rice-shaped pasta, and it makes a nice change from a rice pilaf dish. Garlic shoots (literally the shoot of the garlic bulb, available in spring and early summer) may pose a bit of a challenge when seeking them out. Farmers' markets and upscale grocery stores are your best bet, but if you come up empty-handed in your search, substitute fresh asparagus, which has a similar flavor. A white Burgundy, a dry French wine made from the Chardonnay grape, makes a crisp contrast to the cream in the sauce and highlights the richness of the fish.

Oven-Baked Salmon with Picholine Olive Sauce

Serves 6

PICHOLINE SAUCE
2 cloves garlic, chopped
1 shallot, chopped
1 cup dry vermouth
$^1/_2$ cup chicken stock (page 184) or fish stock (page 184)
$^1/_3$ cup chopped picholine olives
1 cup heavy whipping cream
2 teaspoons chopped fresh thyme
Salt and freshly ground black pepper

3-pound side of salmon, boned and skinned
1 tablespoon unsalted butter
$^1/_2$ cup dry white wine
1 tablespoon chopped fresh tarragon
Salt and freshly ground black pepper

Thyme sprigs, for garnish

Preheat the oven to 400°F. Thoroughly grease a sheet pan.

To prepare the sauce, combine the garlic, shallot, and vermouth in a saucepan over high heat, and reduce until about $^1/_4$ cup of liquid remains, 5 to 6 minutes. Add the stock and reduce until about $^1/_2$ cup of liquid remains, about 4 minutes. Add the olives, cream, and thyme, and reduce until the sauce is thick and coats the back of a spoon, about 5 minutes longer. Season to taste with salt and pepper. Keep warm until you are ready to serve.

To prepare the salmon, place it on the sheet pan. Dot the salmon with the butter, then sprinkle with the wine and tarragon. Season well with salt and pepper. Bake for about 12 minutes, until just cooked through. To serve, slide the salmon onto a serving platter, drizzle with the some of the sauce, and garnish with thyme sprigs. Serve warm, with the extra sauce on the side.

65

Orzo with Fried Shallots

Serves 6

1 pound orzo
1 teaspoon extra virgin olive oil
3 tablespoons unsalted butter
4 shallots, julienned
3 cloves garlic, chopped
4 scallions, both white and green parts, thinly sliced
Salt and freshly ground black pepper

Bring a large pot of salted water to a boil. Add the orzo and cook until al dente, about 5 minutes. Drain well, then toss with the oil; set aside.

Heat the butter in a large sauté pan over medium heat until melted and bubbling. Add the shallots and cook until they start to brown, 3 to 4 minutes. Add the garlic and orzo, toss well, and cook just until the pasta is warm. Remove the pan from the heat, add the scallions, and season to taste with salt and pepper. Transfer to a serving platter and serve warm.

Oven-Roasted Garlic Shoots with Lemon Olive Oil

Serves 6

2 teaspoons extra virgin olive
18 fresh garlic shoots
Sea salt and freshly ground black pepper
2 teaspoons finely grated lemon zest
1 tablespoon lemon olive oil (optional)

Preheat the oven to 425°F. Rub a sheet pan with the extra virgin olive oil.

Arrange the garlic shoots in a single layer on the sheet pan. Season with sea salt and pepper. Roast the garlic shoots for about 5 minutes, until crisp-tender.

Transfer the garlic shoots to a serving platter, sprinkle with the lemon zest, and drizzle with the lemon olive oil. Serve warm.

Cook One:

Cook the orzo.
Prep the garlic shoots and place on a sheet pan.
Finish the olive sauce and keep warm.
Roast the garlic shoots.
Plate the garlic shoots.

Cook Two:

Start making the olive sauce.
Season the salmon and bake.
Finish the orzo.
Plate, sauce, and garnish the salmon and orzo.
Open and pour the wine.

Menu 16:

Pan-Seared Sea Bass with Caramelized Fennel

Croutons with Pecorino Romano

We love to serve this in the early part of the spring when the weather is still a bit hit-and-miss. On those evenings when sunny spring days seem a long way off, nothing cozies up a small dinner party like this sumptuous dish. When plating the sea bass, we place one cheesy crouton on the bottom of a pasta plate, gently set a fillet on top of the crouton, and then finish the dish with two pieces of caramelized fennel and a ladle of the warm, tasty broth. In the recipe, you will see that we have you make two croutons per person— because one never seems to be enough! A Sauvignon Blanc with citrus and herbal notes adds just the right finishing touch to the menu.

Pan-Seared Sea Bass with Caramelized Fennel

Serves 6

3 tablespoons extra virgin olive oil
2 large bulbs fennel, cut into 6 wedges, with 1 tablespoon chopped greens reserved
6 (6-ounce) sea bass fillets
Salt and freshly ground black pepper
$1/2$ cup all-purpose flour
3 cloves garlic, chopped
$1/2$ cup dry white wine
1 tablespoon tarragon vinegar or white wine vinegar
1 cup fish stock (page 184) or chicken stock (page 184)
3 tablespoons unsalted butter

Preheat the oven to 425°F.

To prepare the fennel, heat 2 tablespoon of the olive oil in a roasting pan set over high heat until smoking hot. Add the fennel and cook, without stirring, until it starts to brown, 2 to 3 minutes. Set the pan in the oven and roast the fennel for about 40 minutes, until fork-tender.

About 10 minutes before the fennel is done, begin preparing the fish. Heat the remaining 1 tablespoon olive oil in a large ovenproof sauté pan over high heat until smoking hot. Season the fillets with salt and pepper and dredge them in the flour. Place the fillets in the pan and sear well, 2 to 3 minutes per side. Set the pan in the oven and roast the fish for 5 to 6 minutes depending on the thickness, until it is just cooked through.

When the fish goes in the oven, remove the roasting pan with the fennel, transfer the fennel to a plate, and keep warm. Set the roasting pan over high heat, add the garlic, and sauté for about 1 minute. Add the reserved fennel greens and the wine, and cook for about 2 minutes to deglaze the pan. Add the vinegar, stock, and butter, and bring just to a boil. Season the broth to taste with salt and pepper.

67

(continued)

(continued from page 67)

To serve, place each fillet in a large shallow bowl and set 2 pieces of fennel on top of each fillet. Divide the broth among the bowls. Serve hot.

Cook One:

Prep the fennel.

Sear the fennel and roast in the oven.

Remove the fennel from the oven, lower heat to make croutons, and finish preparing the sauce.

Plate and garnish the fish.

Cook Two:

Prep the sauce ingredients.

Make the croutons.

Sear the fish and finish in the oven.

Open and serve the wine.

Croutons with Pecorino Romano

Serves 6

2 tablespoons extra virgin olive oil
12 ($^1/_2$-inch-thick) slices thick crusted bread, such as ciabatta
1 head garlic, roasted (see page 187)
Finely grated zest of 1 lemon
1 tablespoon chopped flat-leaf parsley
$^3/_4$ cup finely grated Pecorino Romano cheese

Preheat the oven to 350°F.

Drizzle a sheet pan with the olive oil. Set the slices of bread in a single layer in the oil, then flip them over. Mash the roasted garlic with a fork, then spread it over the slices. Combine the lemon zest, parsley, and cheese in a small bowl, mix well, and sprinkle it evenly over the bread slices. Bake the croutons for about 15 minutes, until the bread is golden brown and the cheese is melted. Serve warm.

Menu 17:

Herb-Encrusted Northwest Sea Bass with Green Peppercorn Butter Sauce

White Bean Purée

Fresh Peas with Crème Fraîche

We like serving this menu plated instead of serving family style in three separate serving dishes. As you arrange each element on the plate, you'll see how prettily the contrasting colors and textures come together, and the aroma will tantalize your palate. Begin the plating with a layer of the creamy white bean purée scented simply with garlic and extra virgin olive oil. Next, place the aromatic, tender seared fish fillets that have been generously coated with fresh herbs over the purée. Lightly sautéed fresh peas nestled next to the fillets add another layer of springtime color. For a final touch of lively spice, lightly drizzle the buttery, lemon-tinged sauce over the fish to complete your masterpiece. No beautifully prepared meal is complete without a carefully chosen wine. One of our favorite choices for this menu is a bone-dry Gewürztraminer to add yet another layer of spice.

Herb-Encrusted Northwest Sea Bass with Green Peppercorn Butter Sauce

Serves 6

6 (6-ounce) Oregon sea bass fillets or other mild white fish
2 tablespoons chopped fresh basil
2 tablespoons chopped fresh thyme
2 tablespoons chopped fresh tarragon
3 tablespoons extra virgin olive oil
Salt and freshly ground black pepper

GREEN PEPPERCORN BUTTER SAUCE
1 cup dry white wine
$1/4$ cup white wine vinegar
2 cloves garlic, chopped
1 shallot, chopped
1 cup cold unsalted butter, diced
Juice and finely grated zest of 1 lemon
1 tablespoon crushed green peppercorns
Salt and freshly ground black pepper

1 lemon, sliced, for garnish
Basil, thyme, or tarragon sprigs, for garnish

Preheat the oven to 400°F.

To prepare the sea bass, place the fillets in a large baking dish. Combine the basil, thyme, tarragon, and oil in a bowl, and pour over the fillets. Refrigerate for about 30 minutes to marinate.

Meanwhile, prepare the sauce. Combine the wine, vinegar, garlic, and shallot in a saucepan over high heat and reduce until about $1/4$ cup of liquid remains, about 5 minutes. Decrease the heat to medium-low, and then slowly add the butter and whisk until smooth. Add the lemon juice and zest and peppercorns. Season to taste with salt and pepper. Keep warm (but not hot) until you are ready to serve.

To cook the fish, heat a very large, ovenproof sauté pan over high heat until very hot. Season the fillets with salt and pepper, add to the pan, and sear well, about 3 minutes per side. Set the pan in the oven and roast the fish for 6 to 7 minutes, until just cooked through.

Place the fillets on a serving platter, drizzle with the warm sauce, and garnish with lemon slices and herb sprigs. Serve warm.

Cook One:

Cook the white beans.

Make the reduction for the peppercorn sauce.

Finish the sauce and keep warm.

Just as the fish is removed from the oven, cook the peas.

Plate the peas and beans.

Cook Two:

Prepare and marinate the fish.

Roast the garlic.

Finish the bean purée and keep warm.

Season and sear the fish and finish in the oven.

Plate and garnish the fish.

Open and pour the wine.

White Bean Purée

Serves 6

2 cups cooked cannellini beans or other white beans (see page 187), kept warm

1 head garlic, roasted (see page 187)

2 cloves garlic, chopped

$1/3$ cup extra virgin olive oil

$1/2$ cup vegetable stock (page 186)

Salt and freshly ground black pepper

Combine the warm beans and garlic in the bowl of a food processor and process until smooth. With the machine running, slowly add the oil and then the stock and process until smooth. Season to taste with salt and pepper. Transfer to a serving bowl, and serve warm.

Fresh Peas with Crème Fraîche

Serves 6

1 tablespoon unsalted butter

2 cups freshly shelled peas

1 clove garlic, chopped

1 tablespoon chopped fresh chives

$1/2$ cup crème fraîche (page 187)

Salt and freshly ground black pepper

Fresh chives, for garnish

Heat the butter in a large sauté pan over high heat until melted and bubbling. Add the peas and sauté for about 3 minutes. Add the garlic and the chives, and sauté for about 1 minute. Add the crème fraîche, and cook just until heated through. Season to taste with salt and pepper. Transfer to a serving bowl, and garnish with fresh chives. Serve warm.

Sturgeon Dredged in Seasoned Mushroom Flour

Menu 18:

Sturgeon Dredged in Seasoned Mushroom Flour

Pasta Tossed with Wild Mushrooms

Spinach Salad with Dried Cherry–Port Dressing

This flavorful menu is a study in versatility, adapting well to both casual and more formal settings. Served family-style, it fits well into a relaxed-paced meal. When served in courses, your dinner instantly becomes more elegant, with each dish its own delicious focal point. When choosing dried mushrooms for the dredging flour, we like to find a mixture of wild mushrooms, but of course you can use just one type. If sturgeon is not in season, try another meaty fish like halibut or salmon. For the pasta, use whatever seasonal wild mushroom looks best; if the wild mushrooms are not so great, then try using domestic mushrooms along with some reconstituted dried mushrooms. If you prefer, you can use dried cranberries instead of cherries in the spinach salad dressing; either fruit marries well with the intensity of the port. With this menu we serve a full-bodied zinfandel that is soft in the finish.

Sturgeon Dredged in Seasoned Mushroom Flour

Serves 6

6 (6-ounce) sturgeon fillets
Kosher salt
$^1/_2$ ounce dried wild mushrooms
2 teaspoons dried oregano
2 teaspoons dried thyme
1 teaspoon freshly ground black pepper
1 tablespoon extra virgin olive oil
2 tablespoons lemon olive oil (optional)
1 tablespoon chopped fresh thyme or oregano, for garnish

Preheat the oven to 400°F.

Season the sturgeon fillets with salt; set aside. In an electric spice or coffee grinder, combine the mushrooms, dried oregano, and dried thyme, and grind to a powder. Transfer the mixture to a small bowl, add the pepper, and mix well. Place on a plate. Dredge the fillets in the mushroom flour to coat well.

Heat the olive oil in a large, ovenproof sauté pan over high heat until very hot. Add the fillets and sear well, about 2 minutes per side. Set the pan in the oven and roast the fish until just cooked through, 8 to 10 minutes depending on the thickness of the fillets.

To serve, place each fillet on a plate, drizzle with lemon olive oil, and garnish with chopped fresh thyme or oregano. Serve hot.

Pasta Tossed with Wild Mushrooms

Serves 6

1 pound fettuccine
$^1/_4$ cup extra virgin olive oil
3 cups sliced wild mushrooms, such as chanterelles, morels, or porcini
$^1/_2$ onion, minced
2 cloves garlic, chopped
1 cup dry sherry
1 $^1/_2$ cups mushroom stock (page 185) or chicken stock (page 184)
$^1/_4$ cup chopped fresh basil
Salt and freshly ground black pepper

Bring a large pot of salted water to a boil. Add the fettuccine and cook until al dente, 8 to 10 minutes. Drain well; set aside.

Heat 1 tablespoon of the oil in a large sauté pan over high heat until hot. Add the mushrooms and sauté until they start to soften, about 3 minutes. Add the onion and garlic and sauté for about 1 minute. Add the sherry and cook until the liquid has reduced and the mixture is almost dry, 3 to 5 minutes. Add the stock and reduce until about $^3/_4$ cup remains. Add the basil, pasta, and the remaining 3 tablespoons olive oil, and toss to coat. Season to taste with salt and pepper. Serve warm.

Cook One:

Make the mushroom flour.

Clean the spinach, place in a bowl, cover, and refrigerate.

Cook the fettuccine, drain, and toss with oil.

Make the pasta sauce.

Heat the salad dressing and toss with the spinach.

Plate and garnish the salad.

Cook Two:

Reheat the oven.

Slice the wild mushrooms for the pasta.

Chop the herbs and garlic for all three recipes.

Make the dressing for the spinach salad.

Dredge and sear the fish, and place it in the oven.

When the fish is removed from the oven, toss the pasta with the sauce.

Plate and garnish the fish and pasta.

Spinach Salad with Dried Cherry–Port Dressing

Serves 6

$^1/_2$ cup dried cherries
$^1/_2$ cup port
3 shallots, chopped
2 cloves garlic, chopped
1 teaspoon Dijon mustard
$^1/_4$ cup sherry vinegar
$^3/_4$ cup extra virgin olive oil
Salt and freshly ground black pepper
2 bunches spinach (about $^3/_4$ pound), rinsed well, spun dry, and stems removed
$^1/_2$ cup toasted hazelnuts (see page 188), coarsely chopped
2 ounces blue cheese, crumbled

To make the dressing, combine the cherries, port, shallots, and garlic in a saucepan over high heat and cook until the wine has reduced and the mixture is almost dry, about 4 minutes. Let cool, and then transfer to a food processor. Add the mustard and vinegar, and process. With the motor running, slowly add the olive oil and process until smooth and emulsified. Season to taste with salt and pepper. Transfer to a saucepan over medium-high heat and bring to a boil.

To serve, place the spinach in a large bowl, pour the dressing over the spinach, and toss well. Distribute the salad among six plates and top with the hazelnuts and blue cheese. Serve warm.

73

Menu 19:

Sturgeon with a Horseradish Crust and Watercress Aïoli

Risotto with Sautéed Zucchini and Fresh Corn

Trying to pull off this menu alone would stress out even the most experienced hosts. It's not that any one dish is overly challenging to prepare; when tackled separately, the recipes are fairly easy. The difficulty comes when both recipes need attention at the same time, stretching your culinary resources to the limit. Kitchen teamwork really comes into play here. Cooking side-by-side gives you the freedom to serve a menu like this one, with dishes that need to be cooked in unison. And as a bonus, as you get to spend time with the person joining you in the kitchen, you will also be amazed at what you can create together.

Sturgeon with a Horseradish Crust and Watercress Aïoli

Serves 6

WATERCRESS AÏOLI
Juice and finely grated zest of 1 lemon
1 tablespoon Dijon mustard
2 tablespoons white wine vinegar
2 oil- or salt-packed anchovy fillets
2 cloves garlic, chopped
1 large egg yolk
4 dashes of Worcestershire sauce
4 dashes of Tabasco sauce
3/4 cup extra virgin olive oil
1 bunch watercress (about 1/4 pound), rinsed well and spun dry
Salt and freshly ground black pepper

6 (6-ounce) sturgeon fillets
Salt and freshly ground black pepper
1 1/2 cups finely grated fresh horseradish
1/2 cup finely shredded Parmesan cheese
2 tablespoons extra virgin olive oil

Preheat the oven to 425°F.

To prepare the aïoli, combine the lemon juice and zest, mustard, vinegar, anchovies, garlic, and egg yolk in a food processor and purée for about 30 seconds. Add the Worcestershire sauce and Tabasco. With the motor running, slowly add the oil and process until thick and emulsified. Add the watercress and process until smooth. Transfer the aïoli to a bowl and refrigerate until you are ready to serve.

To prepare the sturgeon, place the fillets on a flat work surface and season well with salt and pepper. Combine the horseradish and cheese in a bowl and mix well. Pat about $1/3$ cup of the horseradish mixture on top of each fillet. Heat the olive oil in a very large nonstick oven-proof sauté pan over high heat until very hot. Add the fillets horseradish side down and cook until brown, 2 to 3 minutes per side. Set the pan in the oven and roast the fillets just until cooked through, 10 to 12 minutes.

Transfer the fillets to a serving platter and top each with a dollop of the aïoli. Serve warm, with the remaining aïoli on the side.

Cook One:

Prep the vegetables for the risotto.

Make the horseradish crust.

Make the risotto, enlisting the help of Cook Two as the arm grows weary while stirring.

Plate the risotto.

Cook Two:

Make the aïoli.

Encrust the sturgeon, sear, and finish cooking in the oven.

Plate and sauce the sturgeon.

Open and pour the wine.

Risotto with Sautéed Zucchini and Fresh Corn

Serves 6

1 tablespoon extra virgin olive oil
2 cloves garlic, chopped
1 shallot, chopped
1 cup arborio rice
3 cups vegetable stock (page 186) or chicken stock (page 184)
1 cup fresh corn kernels (about 1 ear)
1 small zucchini, cut into small dice
1 yellow summer squash, cut into small dice
1 tablespoon chopped fresh tarragon
$1/2$ cup diced fontina cheese
Salt and freshly ground black pepper

Heat the oil in a large saucepan over medium-high heat until hot. Add the garlic and shallot, and sauté for about 1 minute. Add the rice and sauté until the rice becomes opaque, 2 to 3 minutes. Add enough of the hot stock to just cover the rice, about 2 cups, and cook, stirring constantly, until the stock has been absorbed, about 4 minutes. Add another 1 cup of stock and continue cooking, stirring constantly, until the stock has been absorbed, about 4 minutes. Continue adding the stock 1 cup at a time and cooking until all of the stock has been absorbed and the rice is al dente, about 20 minutes total. Add the corn, zucchini, yellow squash, and tarragon, and cook, stirring constantly, just until the squashes are tender, 2 to 3 minutes. Remove the pan from the heat. Add the cheese and stir until melted. Season to taste with salt and pepper. Serve in pasta plates or large, shallow bowls. Serve warm.

Menu 20:

Sweet-and-Spicy Curry-Grilled Tuna
Gingered Vegetable–Rice Noodle Slaw

We always manage to stretch the grilling season for as long as possible, whether it means John is manning the grill while hunkered down under an umbrella in a chilly downpour, or he's out in the sweltering heat while the rest of us are sipping margaritas under a garden umbrella. This menu is ideal for the heat of the summer, because it is fresh, spicy, and beautiful, and yet not too heavy for a warm evening. Remember that tuna should be cooked to no more than medium-rare, otherwise it becomes tough and dry. When you prepare the noodle slaw, it is best to have the vegetables and dressing prepped before you soak and cook the noodles. However, if your timing is not perfect and your noodles sit too long and stick together, don't panic—simply rinse them under cold water and they'll separate like magic.

Sweet- and-Spicy Curry-Grilled Tuna

Serves 6

SWEET-AND-SPICY GRILL SAUCE
$1/_4$ cup hot curry powder
$1/_2$ cup mirin
1 tablespoon peeled, finely grated fresh ginger
2 cloves garlic, minced
Juice and finely grated zest of 2 limes
$1/_4$ cup rice vinegar
2 tablespoons chopped fresh cilantro
$3/_4$ cup Major Grey's chutney
3 tablespoons soy sauce

6 (6-ounce) ahi tuna fillets
Salt and freshly ground black pepper
1 large mango, peeled and diced

Cilantro sprigs, for garnish

Oil the grill and prepare a medium-hot fire. If you are using a gas grill, preheat on medium-high. If you are using a charcoal grill, let the coals burn until they are covered with gray ash. The fire is medium-hot when you can hold your hand over the grill for no longer than 5 seconds.

To prepare the sauce, heat a dry sauté pan over medium-high heat until hot. Add the curry and cook, stirring continuously, until fragrant and lightly toasted, about 2 minutes. Add the mirin and cook for about 2 minutes. Transfer to a bowl and add the ginger, garlic, lime juice and zest, vinegar, cilantro, chutney, and soy sauce. Refrigerate until you are ready to use it.

To prepare the tuna, place about 1 cup of the sauce on a large plate or platter (you can save any remaining sauce for another use for up to 2 weeks in the refrigerator). Season the fillets with salt and pepper, and dredge them in the sauce. Place the fillets on the grill and cook just until medium-rare, about 3 minutes per side, depending on the thickness of the fillets.

To serve, place the fillets on a serving platter, top with the mango, and garnish with cilantro sprigs. Serve hot.

Gingered Vegetable–Rice Noodle Slaw

Serves 6

1 (1-pound) package dried thin rice noodles

1 red onion, julienned

1 large carrot, peeled and julienned

$^1/_2$ pound small French green beans, trimmed, blanched, and shocked (see page 188)

3 cloves garlic, minced

3 tablespoon peeled, grated fresh ginger

Juice and finely grated zest of 1 lime

Juice and finely grated zest of 1 orange

$^1/_2$ teaspoon orange oil

2 tablespoons sesame oil

$^1/_4$ cup rice vinegar

$^3/_4$ cup vegetable oil, preferably canola

Soy sauce

In a large bowl, combine the noodles with enough hot water to cover, and let stand for about 10 minutes.

In a stockpot over high heat, bring about 8 cups of salted water to a rolling boil. Drain the noodles, then add them to the boiling water and cook until tender, about 2 minutes. Drain the noodles well and transfer to a large bowl. Add the onion, carrot, and green beans, and toss well; set aside.

In a small bowl, whisk together the garlic, ginger, lime juice, orange juice and zest, orange oil, sesame oil, and rice vinegar. While whisking, slowly add the vegetable oil, and whisk until smooth. Season to taste with soy sauce, and mix well. Pour the dressing over the salad and toss well. Let the salad marinate at room temperature for at least 30 minutes before serving.

Cook One:

Soak the noodles.

Cook the noodles.

Make the grill sauce.

Grill the tuna.

Plate and garnish the tuna.

Cook Two:

Prep the vegetables for the slaw.

Finish preparing the slaw.

Oil and light the grill.

Plate and garnish the slaw.

Open and pour the wine.

Menu 21:

Niçoise Salad

It doesn't happen often in Portland, but on those days when it's just too hot to think about cooking, much less eating, this salad is the answer. Crisp, cold vegetables, olive oil–infused tuna, and a piquant dressing come together in a refreshing palette of color and taste that beckons your appetite. A slightly chilled bottle of Beaujolais will frame this composition perfectly.

Cook One:

Blanch and shock the green beans.
Make the dressing.
Compose the salad together.

Cook Two:

Cook the potatoes and hard-boil the eggs.
Prep the remaining vegetables.
Compose the salad together.

Niçoise Salad

Serves 6

2 tablespoons sherry vinegar
2 cloves garlic, minced
1 tablespoon Dijon mustard
$^1/_3$ cup extra virgin olive oil
Salt and freshly ground black pepper
18 ounces high-quality olive oil–packed canned tuna
3 ripe tomatoes, cut into wedges
$^1/_2$ pound green beans, trimmed, blanched, and
　　　shocked (see page 188)
12 red potatoes, cooked (see page 188) and quartered
6 hard-boiled eggs, peeled and halved
6 radishes, thinly sliced
$^1/_3$ cup Niçoise olives or other cured black olives

To prepare the dressing, whisk together the vinegar, garlic, and mustard in a small bowl. While whisking, slowly add the olive oil and whisk until smooth and emulsified. Season to taste with salt and pepper; set aside.

To prepare the salad, divide the tuna among six entrée plates. Distribute the tomatoes, green beans, potatoes, eggs, radishes, and olives over the tuna. Drizzle the dressing over the salads. Serve immediately.

Menu 22:

Saffron-Scented Fish Chowder with Parmesan Tuiles

Romaine Hearts with Warm Brie Dressing

Don't let the term "chowder" fool you into thinking this is lunchtime fare. This elegant soup with a silky broth and sublime flavor will woo even the most discerning guests. And working together, you can serve it with all the skill of practiced chefs. You can make the broth base and the salad dressing the day before your dinner party. Just before serving, simply heat, plate, and garnish. And once you join the table, the adulation and murmurs of contentment will be your reward. With the mild fish and the subtle anise flavor of the fennel in the soup, we enjoy a citrusy wine, such as Sauvignon Blanc.

Saffron-Scented Fish Chowder with Parmesan Tuiles

Serves 6

1 tablespoon extra virgin olive oil
1 medium onion, diced
1 large bulb fennel, cored and diced, with 1 teaspoon chopped greens reserved
3 cloves garlic, chopped
3 stalks celery, diced
1/2 cup dry sherry
1/2 cup Madeira
8 cups fish stock (page 184)
1 teaspoon chopped fresh tarragon
1 teaspoon chopped fresh flat-leaf parsley
1/2 teaspoon saffron threads
4 Yukon Gold potatoes, peeled and diced
1 1/2 pounds seasonal white fish fillets, cut into large dice
Salt and freshly ground black pepper
1 cup finely grated Parmesan cheese
Flat-leaf parsley sprigs, for garnish

To prepare the chowder, heat the oil in a large stockpot over high heat until hot. Add the onion, fennel bulb, garlic, and celery, and sauté for 3 to 4 minutes. Add the sherry and Madeira, and reduce over high heat until about 1/4 cup of liquid remains. Add the stock, reserved fennel greens, tarragon, and parsley, and cook until reduced by about one-half, about 1 hour. Strain through a fine sieve, discarding the vegetables. Pour the soup back into the pot, add the saffron and potatoes, and simmer over medium heat until the potatoes are tender, 10 to 15 minutes. Add the fish and cook just until the fish is cooked through, about 4 minutes. Season to taste with salt and pepper. Keep warm.

To prepare the tuiles, preheat the oven to 425°F. Oil a sheet pan well. Sprinkle the Parmesan cheese onto the pan to make six rustic circles. Bake until melted and lightly brown, about 3 minutes. Let the tuiles cool on the pan until crispy, about 2 minutes.

To serve, ladle the soup into bowls and top each with a tuile. Garnish with parsley sprigs. Serve hot.

Cook One:

Make the broth.
Make the tuiles.
Strain the broth.
Add the potatoes and the fish to the broth.
Plate and garnish the soup.

Cook Two:

Make the salad dressing.
Clean and prep the lettuce.
Plate the lettuce.
When the fish and potatoes are done, dress the lettuce.
Open and serve the wine.

Romaine Hearts with Warm Brie Dressing

Serves 6

WARM BRIE DRESSING
1 cup dry white wine
3 cloves garlic, chopped
1 shallot chopped
1 tablespoon sherry vinegar
1 cup heavy whipping cream
4 ounces ripe Brie, diced
Finely grated zest of 1 lemon
$1/2$ teaspoon lemon oil (optional)
Salt and finely grated black pepper

3 hearts romaine lettuce, rinsed well and halved
$1/2$ cup toasted breadcrumbs (page 181)

To make the dressing, combine the wine, garlic, shallot, and vinegar in a saucepan over high heat and reduce until about $1/4$ cup of liquid remains, about 5 minutes. Add the cream and cook, stirring occasionally, until the dressing starts to thicken, about 5 minutes. Add the Brie and whisk until melted. Add the lemon zest and lemon oil, and whisk until smooth. Season to taste with salt and pepper. Keep warm, but not hot, until you are ready to serve.

To serve, place each lettuce half on a plate. Drizzle with the warm dressing and sprinkle with the breadcrumbs. Serve immediately.

Menu 23:

Crab and Sweet Potato Stew

Sautéed Baby Artichokes with Tarragon

We use this menu to straddle winter's departure and the entrance of spring. The stew isn't your typical hearty winter fare. Instead, it's much more distinctive than the name may lead you to believe. Each bowl of the light, delicate broth, enriched with a touch of crème fraîche, is studded with bits of seared sweet potatoes and adorned with a fresh crab relish. Visiting the market in the early spring, we were inspired by the baby artichokes and knew they were just the right vegetable to accompany the heavenly entrée and give the menu a hint of spring.

Crab and Sweet Potato Stew

Serves 6

8 slices pancetta, diced
1 tablespoon extra virgin olive oil
1 large onion, diced
3 sweet potatoes, peeled and diced
1 cup dry sherry
3 cups chicken stock (page 184)
1 1/2 pounds fresh crabmeat
1 bunch scallions, both green and white parts, thinly sliced
2 teaspoons chopped fresh flat-leaf parsley
1 cup crème fraîche (page 181)
Salt and freshly ground black pepper

Heat a large, deep sauté pan over medium heat until hot. Add the pancetta and cook until crispy, about 3 minutes. Using a slotted spoon, transfer the pancetta to paper towels to drain, reserving the drippings in the pan. Add the oil and onion to the pan, and cook the onion over medium heat, without stirring, until they start to brown, about 5 minutes. Add the sweet potatoes and cook again, without stirring, until brown, about 5 minutes. Stir, then add the sherry and reduce until about 1/2 cup of liquid remains, about 5 minutes. Add the chicken stock and cook until the sweet potatoes are tender, about 10 minutes.

Meanwhile, combine the crab, scallions, and parsley in a bowl, and mix well; refrigerate the mixture until you are ready to serve.

When the sweet potatoes are tender, gently fold in the crème fraîche, and season to taste with salt and pepper.

To serve, ladle the stew into shallow pasta bowls, then distribute the crab and crispy pancetta over the top. Serve warm.

Sautéed Baby Artichokes with Tarragon

Serves 6

2 tablespoons extra virgin olive oil
9 baby artichokes, trimmed, stems removed, and halved
3 cloves garlic, minced
2 anchovy fillets, minced
3/4 cup dry sherry
1 tablespoon chopped fresh tarragon
Juice and finely grated zest of 1 lemon
1 tablespoon tarragon vinegar or white wine vinegar
2 tablespoons unsalted butter
Salt and freshly ground black pepper
Lemon zest strips, for garnish

Heat the oil in a very large sauté pan over high heat until smoking hot. Add the artichokes and cook, without stirring, until they just start to brown, about 3 minutes. Add the garlic and sauté for about 1 minute. Add the anchovies and sherry, and reduce until about 1/4 cup of liquid remains, about 4 minutes. Add the tarragon, lemon juice and zest, and vinegar, and toss with the artichokes. Add the butter and cook just until the artichokes are tender, 3 to 4 minutes longer. Season to taste with salt and pepper.

Place on a serving platter and garnish with strips of lemon zest. Serve warm or at room temperature.

Cook One:

Prep the vegetables for the stew.
Make the stew base.
Toss the crab with the herbs.
Plate and garnish the stew.

Cook Two:

Prep the artichokes.
Cook the artichokes.
Plate and garnish the artichokes.
Open and pour the wine.

Menu 24:

Winter Squash Bisque with Lobster
Shaved Fennel and Blood Orange Salad

For this bisque, you must begin with live lobsters, which need to be prepped as humanely as possible. With this in mind, our preferred method for dealing with them is very quickly with a sharp knife (see recipe) instead of placing them live in boiling water. We have served variations of this salad at the Bistro, usually in the middle of winter to provide a taste of culinary sunshine. To get the fennel as thin as we do at the restaurant, you really need to use a mandoline, a slicing tool you can find at every price range, from 15 dollars for a basic, serviceable model to 125 dollars for a sleek stainless-steel version. This recipe calls for soaking the fennel in ice water after slicing it, which makes it especially crisp. The deep ruby color and juicy sweetness of the blood oranges make a beautiful contrast, but if that variety is not available, another seasonal orange will work just fine.

Winter Squash Bisque with Lobster

Serves 6

1 tablespoon extra virgin olive oil
2 cloves garlic, chopped
1 large onion, diced
6 cups fish stock (page 184) or chicken stock (page 184)
2 (1- to 2-pound) live lobsters
2 small or 1 large butternut squash, peeled and diced
1 tablespoon chopped fresh thyme
1 1/2 cups heavy whipping cream
1 tablespoon soy sauce
2 teaspoons orange juice concentrate
Salt and freshly ground black pepper
1/2 cup crème fraîche (page 181) or sour cream,
    for garnish
Thyme sprigs, for garnish

Heat the oil in a stockpot over high heat until hot. Add the garlic and onion, and sauté for about 2 minutes. Add the stock and bring to a boil. While the stock is coming to a boil, prepare the lobsters. Using a very sharp knife, make a very deep cut in each lobster in the middle of the head. When the stock is boiling, add the lobsters, cover the pot with a lid, and cook the lobsters just until they are cooked through, about 10 minutes. Remove the lobsters from the stock, and let them cool. Add the squash to the stock and cook over medium heat until tender, about 10 minutes.

Once the lobsters are cool enough to handle, remove the meat from the claws and tail. Dice the meat and set aside. Return the shells to the soup, add the chopped thyme and cream, and simmer over medium heat for about 20 minutes. Strain the soup through a fine-mesh sieve into another pan, pressing the squash through the sieve, and gently warm over medium heat. Add the soy sauce and orange juice concentrate, mix well, and season to taste with salt and pepper.

To serve, divide the reserved lobster meat among six bowls. Ladle the hot soup over the lobster meat, and garnish with a dollop of crème fraîche and thyme sprigs.

Shaved Fennel and Blood Orange Salad

Serves 6

3 bulbs fennel, trimmed, with 1 tablespoon chopped greens reserved
4 blood oranges, sectioned
Finely grated zest of 1 blood orange
2 tablespoons white wine vinegar
1 clove garlic, minced
2/3 cup extra virgin olive oil
Salt and freshly ground black pepper
2 ounces Pecorino Romano cheese, shaved

Using a mandoline, shave the fennel into very thin slices, being sure to avoid the core of the fennel. In a very large bowl, cover the fennel with ice and water, and soak for about 30 minutes; drain well.

Combine the fennel, reserved fennel greens, and orange sections in a serving bowl, and toss together. In a small bowl, whisk together the orange zest, vinegar, and garlic. While whisking, slowly add the olive oil and whisk until very smooth. Season to taste with salt and pepper. Pour the dressing over the fennel mixture and toss well. Divide the salad among 6 serving plates. Garnish with the cheese, and serve immediately.

Cook One:

Prep the lobster.

Peel and dice the squash.

When the lobsters are cooked through, remove from the stock and extract the meat.

Dice the lobster meat.

Section the oranges.

Strain and season the soup.

Plate and garnish the soup.

Cook Two:

Prep the garlic and onion, and start the soup.

Add the stock and prepared lobsters to the soup.

Finish preparing the bisque.

Shave the fennel.

Make the salad dressing.

Shave the cheese for the garnish.

Toss, plate, and garnish the salad.

Open and pour the wine.

Menu 25:

Seared Sea Scallops with Herb Crème
Vegetable Hash

When we were developing this menu, we got carried away, adding far too many steps to the herb crème, which made it too complicated and time-consuming. We found ourselves working more with the restaurant in mind, momentarily losing our vision of always trying to create recipes that keep the home chef in the forefront. Stepping back and realizing what we had done to the sauce, we knew that, although it was tasty, you would need an army of cooks to prepare it. Taking a second look, we reworked and simplified the recipe without losing the integrity of our original entrée. When you prepare the scallops, be sure to use ovenproof plates, since the dish is sauced and finished under the broiler. A small spoonful of the colorful vegetable mixture sitting atop the crispy glazed scallops functions as both garnish and side dish. To serve, we always place each hot plate on a charger or larger plate, saving our table and our guests' fingertips from danger.

Seared Sea Scallops with Herb Crème

Serves 6

HERB CRÈME

1 bunch watercress (about $1/4$ pound), rinsed well
　　and spun dry
1 tablespoon chopped fresh chives
1 tablespoon chopped fresh flat-leaf parsley
1 tablespoon chopped fresh tarragon
4 cloves garlic
3 salt-packed anchovy fillets
1 tablespoon drained capers
3 large egg yolks
1 heaping tablespoon Dijon mustard
1 cup softly whipped cream
Salt and freshly ground black pepper

30 fresh sea scallops
Salt and freshly ground black pepper
2 tablespoons extra virgin olive oil

To prepare the herb crème, combine the watercress, chives, parsley, tarragon, garlic, anchovies, capers, and egg yolks in a food processor and process until smooth. Transfer to a large bowl and fold in the whipped cream. Season with salt and pepper and set aside until you are ready to serve.

To prepare the scallops, preheat the broiler. Season the scallops with salt and pepper. Heat the oil in a very large sauté pan over high heat until smoking hot. Add as many of the scallops as will fit without overcrowding the pan and sear well, about 2 minutes per side, then quickly remove from the pan. Continue with the remaining scallops.

Divide the scallops among six ovenproof pasta plates. Distribute the herb crème over the scallops. Set the plates under the broiler, and broil just until the herb crème is lightly browned, about 2 minutes. Serve immediately.

Vegetable Hash

Serves 6

2 tablespoons unsalted butter
1 small onion, minced
1 large carrot, cut into small dice
2 Yukon Gold potatoes, cut into small dice
1 medium zucchini, cut into small dice
1 red bell pepper, cut into small dice
$^1/_2$ cup dry white wine
Salt and freshly ground black pepper
2 teaspoons chopped fresh flat-leaf parsley

Heat the butter in a large sauté pan over medium-high heat until melted and bubbling. Add the onion, carrot, and potatoes, and cook, without stirring, until they start to brown, 3 to 5 minutes. Toss and continue cooking, again without stirring, until brown, 3 to 5 minutes longer. Add the zucchini and pepper, and sauté for about 2 minutes. Add the wine and reduce over high heat until the mixture is just about dry, about 3 minutes. Season to taste with salt and pepper, and continue cooking just until the potatoes are tender, about 2 minutes.

Remove the pan from the heat, add the parsley, and toss well. Transfer to a serving platter, and serve warm.

Cook One:

Make the herb crème.
Sear and plate the scallops.
Sauce and broil the scallops.

Cook Two:

Prep the vegetables for the hash.
Finish the hash and keep warm.
Top the scallops with the hash and serve.

Menu 26:

Grilled Shrimp with Crispy Fried Caper Sauce

Traditional Rice Pilaf

Summer Vegetable Sauté

With our busy life, we find that shrimp makes a great choice for a quick and yummy meal. Once the grill is hot, it's a matter of minutes before dinner is on the table. When we make this marinade and sauce, we're always thrilled to have leftovers, because almost any seafood shines when paired with these flavors of sunny Provence. The most important technique for preparing the simple side dish is patience, which allows the vegetable to cook properly. When we taught this sauté in a hands-on class at our cooking school, we found that people had a hard time resisting the urge to stir. But once they taste the finished dish, they were surprised at how much more flavorful it is when each vegetable is given the time to brown. To continue the theme of Provence, we like to drink a chilled dry Provençal rosé.

Grilled Shrimp with Crispy Fried Caper Sauce

Serves 6

MARINADE
2 cloves garlic, chopped
Juice and finely grated zest of 1 lemon
2 teaspoons dried herbes de Provence
1 teaspoon Dijon mustard
1 teaspoon honey
$1/_3$ cup extra virgin olive oil
Salt and freshly ground black pepper

30 extra-large shrimp, peeled and deveined, tails intact

CRISPY FRIED CAPER SAUCE
$1/_3$ cup extra virgin olive oil
1 tablespoon capers, drained
1 tablespoon white wine vinegar
1 tablespoon dried herbes de Provence
1 teaspoon chopped fresh thyme
Salt and freshly ground black pepper

Soak six large bamboo skewers in water for 10 minutes.

To prepare the marinade, whisk together the garlic, lemon juice and zest, herbs, mustard, and honey in a small bowl. While whisking, slowly add the oil and whisk until smooth. Season to taste with salt and pepper. When the skewers are soaked, place five shrimp on each one and set them in a 9 by 13-inch pan. Pour the marinade over the shrimp and let marinate for 30 minutes.

Meanwhile, to prepare the sauce, heat 2 teaspoons of the oil in a small sauté pan over high heat until smoking hot. Add the capers and cook until the capers start to turn crispy, 2 to 3 minutes. Remove the pan from the heat and let cool. In a small bowl, whisk together the vinegar and herbs. While whisking, slowly add the remaining oil and whisk until smooth. Add the cooled

91

(continued)

(continued from page 91)

capers and season to taste with salt and pepper. Keep at room temperature until you are ready to serve.

Oil the grill and prepare a hot fire. If you are using a gas grill, preheat on high. If you are using a charcoal grill, let the coals burn until they are covered with gray ash. The fire is hot when you can hold your hand over the grill for no longer than 5 seconds.

When the coals are hot, drain the marinade from the shrimp, place the skewers on the hot grill, and grill until the shrimp are just cooked, about 1 minute per side.

Transfer the skewers to a platter and drizzle with some of the caper sauce. Serve hot, with the remaining sauce on the side.

Traditional Rice Pilaf

Serves 6

1 tablespoon unsalted butter
1/2 small onion, minced
2 cloves garlic, chopped
1 1/2 cups long-grain white rice
3 cups chicken stock (page 184)
1 teaspoon salt

Preheat the oven to 350°F.

Heat the butter in a large ovenproof saucepan over medium-high heat until melted and bubbling. Add the onion and garlic, and sauté for about 2 minutes. Add the rice and stir to coat with the butter. Add the chicken stock and salt, and bring to a boil. Cover the pan with a lid, set it in the oven, and cook until the rice is tender, about 30 minutes. Fluff with a fork just before serving. Serve hot.

Summer Vegetable Sauté

Serves 6

1 small eggplant, cubed
2 teaspoons kosher salt
2 tablespoons extra virgin olive oil
1 small onion, diced
3 cloves garlic, chopped
$1/2$ pound button mushrooms, quartered
1 yellow summer squash, cubed
1 zucchini, cubed
2 red bell peppers, roasted, peeled, seeded
(see page 187), and diced
1 cup chopped oil-cured tomatoes,
or 2 large vine-ripened tomatoes, chopped
1 tablespoon chopped fresh thyme
1 tablespoon chopped fresh oregano
Salt and freshly ground black pepper

In a large bowl combine the eggplant with the kosher salt, toss to mix, and let sit for about 10 minutes.

Heat 1 tablespoon of the oil in a large sauté pan over high heat until hot. Add the eggplant and cook, without stirring, until it starts to brown, about 3 minutes. Toss well, add the onion and garlic, and sauté for about 2 minutes, adding more olive oil as needed. Add the mushrooms and cook, again without stirring, until brown, about 3 minutes. Toss well, add the yellow squash and zucchini, and cook, without stirring, for about 3 minutes. Add the roasted peppers, tomatoes, thyme, and oregano, and sauté just until heated through. Season to taste with salt and pepper. Serve warm.

Cook One:

Make the marinade for the shrimp, then marinate the shrimp.

Oil and light the grill.

Make the caper sauce.

Grill the shrimp.

Plate the shrimp.

Cook Two:

Prep the vegetables for the sauté.

Make the rice pilaf.

Cook and finish the sauté.

Plate the pilaf and the sauté.

Open and pour the wine.

93

Menu 27:

Herb-Dressed Seafood Salad

Sweet Onion Rings

We taught a popular summer class that featured entrée salads for warm-weather dining. Included in the lineup was this fabulous salad with a luxurious dressing spiked with fresh herbs. During the class, we showed our students an extra step that takes the dressing from very good to phenomenal, and although it adds another dimension, we didn't include it in the recipe because it isn't critical to the flavor of the finished dish. The secret is to reduce the poaching liquid over high heat until about 2 tablespoons remain, then cool and whisk the intense reduction into the dressing. It is such a simple step, yet we didn't want people to feel pressured for time when faced with this addition to the dressing and abandon the idea of making the salad altogether. Encouraging our students to modify recipes to suit the moment or the season gives them the confidence to venture beyond the boundaries of the recipes. Just like the extra step in the dressing, the onion rings can add a welcome texture, but their omission certainly won't lessen the impact of the meal.

Herb-Dressed Seafood Salad

Serves 6

SEAFOOD
1 pound seasonal fish, such as halibut, diced
1 1/2 pounds extra-large shrimp, peeled and split in half
1 1/2 cups dry white wine
1 clove garlic, chopped
Pinch of saffron
1/4 pound fresh crabmeat

CREAMY HERB DRESSING
1/4 cup white wine vinegar
1 tablespoon Dijon mustard
2 cloves garlic, chopped
1 small shallot, diced
1 large egg yolk
3/4 cup extra virgin olive oil
2 teaspoons chopped fresh thyme
2 teaspoons chopped fresh tarragon
Tabasco sauce
Salt and freshly ground black pepper

2 to 3 heads romaine lettuce, rinsed well, spun dry, and torn into bite-sized pieces
1 head fennel, thinly shaved
1 red onion, julienned

To poach the seafood, combine the fish and shrimp in a large sauté pan. Pour in the wine, then add the garlic and saffron. Set the pan over medium heat and simmer until the fish is just cooked, 4 to 5 minutes, depending on the type of fish. Using a slotted spoon, remove the fish and shrimp from the cooking liquid, transfer to a bowl, and refrigerate until well chilled, about 1 hour. Fold in the crabmeat.

Meanwhile, to make the dressing, combine the vinegar, mustard, garlic, shallot, and egg yolk in a bowl. While whisking, slowly add the oil, and whisk until smooth and emulsified. Add the thyme and tarragon, and season to taste with Tabasco, salt, and pepper. Refrigerate until you are ready to serve.

To assemble the salad, in a large bowl, combine the lettuce, fennel, and onion, and toss. Add enough of the dressing to coat the lettuce leaves, and toss well (save any remaining dressing in the refrigerator for another use). Divide the salad among six large entrée plates, then distribute the chilled seafood over the salads. Serve cold.

Cook One:

Poach the fish and chill.
Make the dressing.
Prep the lettuce and vegetables for the salad.
Dress and plate the salad, and top with the seafood.

Cook Two:

Prep the onions and cover with buttermilk.
Make the seasoned flour.
Fry the onion rings.
Garnish the salads with the onion rings.

Sweet Onion Rings

Serves 6

3 Walla Walla onions, thinly sliced
2 cups buttermilk
2 cups all-purpose flour
2 cups chickpea flour
3 tablespoons smoked paprika
1 tablespoon salt
2 teaspoons freshly ground black pepper
Vegetable oil, for frying

In a bowl, cover the sliced onions with the buttermilk. Let sit for at least 30 minutes, or up to 24 hours.

Combine the flour, chickpea flour, paprika, salt, and pepper in a bowl, and mix well.

Heat about 4 inches of vegetable oil in a large stockpot over high heat until it reaches 350°F. When the oil is hot, drain the onions well, then dredge them in the flour mixture. Place as many of the onions in the oil as will fit without overcrowding the pan, and fry until crispy and golden brown, about 3 minutes. Transfer to paper towels to drain. Continue frying the remaining onions. Serve warm.

Menu 28:

Chicken Roasted in Seasoned Sea Salt

Cabbage Braised with Smoked Paprika and Cumin

After a really busy day, we like to make this menu for dinner, because once we get it started and in the oven we can forget about it for an hour and relax with our kids. Both of these dishes are so fragrant they can really turn your day around. The seasoned sea salt completely permeates the chicken, making it unbelievably moist and tender. Sometimes we cook two chickens at the same time, and then pull the meat off of one to save for later in the week as a garnish for a hearty fall soup or salad. The scent of the cumin and paprika in the cabbage gives off a warm, smoky aroma that elevates that humble vegetable to new heights.

Chicken Roasted in Seasoned Sea Salt

Serves 4

3 cups sea salt
Finely grated zest of 2 lemons
1 tablespoon dried basil
1 tablespoon dried thyme
2 cloves garlic, minced
1 teaspoon freshly ground black pepper
1 (3-pound) roasting chicken

Preheat the oven to 350°F. Combine the sea salt, lemon zest, basil, thyme, garlic, and pepper in a food processor, and process until well blended. Spread the salt mixture over a large sheet of aluminum foil. Place the chicken, breast side down, in the center of the salt. Carefully fold the foil around the chicken and crimp the foil to seal. Set the chicken in a roasting pan and roast for about 1 1/2 hours, until it reaches an internal temperature of 155°F. (To test for doneness, open the foil and insert an instant-read thermometer into the thigh of the chicken.)

Remove the chicken from the oven, carefully open the foil, and brush the salt from the chicken. Slice and serve warm.

Cabbage Braised with Smoked Paprika and Cumin

Serves 6

1 large cabbage
2 tablespoons unsalted butter
1 clove garlic, chopped
1 teaspoon cumin seeds
1 cup vegetable stock (page 186) or chicken stock
　　(page 184)
2 teaspoons smoked paprika
2 tablespoons sherry vinegar
2 teaspoons chopped fresh flat-leaf parsley
Salt and freshly ground black pepper

Cut the cabbage into six wedges, leaving the root end of each piece intact. Heat the butter in a very large sauté pan over medium-high heat until melted and bubbling. Add the garlic and cumin seeds, and sauté for about 2 minutes. Add the cabbage, stock, and paprika, and bring to a boil. Lower the heat to medium, cover, and cook until the cabbage is tender, about 15 minutes. Remove the pan from the heat, add the vinegar and parsley, and season to taste with salt and pepper.

Place the cabbage on a large serving platter, and pour the sauce over the top. Serve warm.

Cook One:

Prep the seasoned sea salt.

About 15 minutes before the chicken is done, cut the cabbage.

Remove the chicken from the oven, brush off the salt, and slice.

Plate the chicken.

Cook Two:

Prepare the foil, add the salt, wrap the chicken, and place in the oven.

Chop the garlic and heat the butter for the cabbage.

Braise the cabbage.

Plate the cabbage.

Menu 29:

Chicken Braised with Seared Oranges, Tomatoes, and Tarragon

Spiced Pan-Fried Green Beans and Chickpeas

Braising takes an inexpensive cut of meat and makes it moist and savory. No matter what you are braising, use an intensely flavored broth for the best results. In this menu, the first step in the chicken's transformation is to dredge it in a rich, nutty chickpea flour (an ingredient you can find at well-stocked grocery stores or specialty markets) before searing. After the chicken has been seared and sprinkled with orange zest, orange halves are added to the hot pan, where the heat draws out the juice and caramelizes it. Deglazing the pan with Madeira comes next, imbuing the sauce with the tempting flavors lifted from the pan. Each of these steps plays an important role in building complexity into the braising liquid and ultimately in the mouthwatering chicken. For us, a kitchen filled with these warm scents typifies our idea of a relaxing, cozy night at home. The aromatic elements of orange, chickpea, Madeira, and tarragon wafting through the house cry out for the deep flavors of a Spanish Tempranillo, a lively, spicy red wine.

Chicken Braised with Seared Oranges, Tomatoes, and Tarragon

Serves 6

2 (2 1/2-pound) fryer chickens, cut into pieces
Salt and freshly ground black pepper
2 cups chickpea flour
2 tablespoons extra virgin olive oil
Finely grated zest of 1 orange
2 oranges, halved
1 cup Madeira
2 cloves garlic, chopped
2 cups chicken stock (page 184)
1 cinnamon stick
3 tomatoes, seeded (see page 188) and cut into
    large dice
1 tablespoon chopped fresh tarragon
1 bunch watercress, rinsed well and spun dry,
    for garnish

Preheat the oven to 375°F.

Season the chicken with salt and pepper, then dredge it in the chickpea flour. Heat the oil in a large, oven-proof sauté pan over high heat until very hot. Add the chicken and brown well, about 3 minutes per side. Sprinkle the chicken with the orange zest. Add the oranges, cut side down, and cook, without stirring, until caramelized, about 3 minutes. Add the Madeira and garlic and reduce until about 1/2 cup of liquid remains, about 4 minutes. Add the chicken stock, cinnamon stick, tomatoes, and tarragon, and bring to a boil. Cover the pan with a lid or foil, set it in the oven, and cook for about 40 minutes, until the chicken is just cooked through. Using a slotted spoon, remove the chicken from the sauce and place on a serving platter. Season the braising liquid to taste with salt and pepper, then strain through a fine-mesh sieve. Pour the sauce over the chicken, and garnish with the watercress. Serve warm.

Spiced Pan-Fried Green Beans and Chickpeas

Serves 6

2 teaspoons vegetable oil

1 pound green beans, trimmed, blanched, and shocked (see page 188)

2 cups cooked chickpeas (see page 187)

2 teaspoons peeled, chopped fresh ginger

1 clove garlic, chopped

1/4 teaspoon five-spice powder

1/2 teaspoon crushed red pepper flakes

Soy sauce

2 teaspoons chopped fresh cilantro, for garnish

Heat the oil in a large sauté pan over high heat until hot. Add the green beans and cook, without stirring, until they start to brown, about 2 minutes. Add the chickpeas, ginger, garlic, and five-spice, and sauté for about 1 minute. Add the pepper flakes, mix well, and season to taste with soy sauce. Place the beans on a serving platter and garnish with the cilantro. Serve warm.

Cook One:

Season and sear the chicken.

Caramelize the oranges.

Finish preparing the braising liquid, and place the chicken in the oven.

Pour two glasses of nicely chilled white wine to share while cooking.

Finish preparing the green beans.

Plate and garnish the green beans.

Cook Two:

Cook the chickpeas.

Blanch and shock the green beans.

Prep the tomatoes for the braising liquid.

Remove the chicken from the oven, and season and strain the braising liquid.

Plate and garnish the chicken.

Open and pour the red wine for dinner.

Menu 30:

Crispy Chicken Medallions with Three-Mustard Sauce

Pappardelle Tossed with Arugula and Spinach

Students at our cooking school regularly request classes with family-friendly recipes. Assuming that our kids have the palates of chefs, they are surprised to learn that Alex and Savannah are just like almost every other American kid, liking anything as long as it's plain and fried. Although we don't have all the answers, we've learned a few tricks to get them to eat a varied and healthy diet (and more so because we are parents rather than because we are chefs). Our kids are more adventuresome at the table when served dishes sauced with sour cream, and a crispy bite always works wonders. These chicken medallions have all the requisite elements for the family table, winning raves from kids and parents alike. The pasta dish provides a way to introduce a vegetable to the menu; just be sure to pick a very mild goat cheese that won't overwhelm timid palates. And by all means, don't tell them it's goat cheese until after dinner!

Crispy Chicken Medallions with Three-Mustard Sauce

Serves 6

6 boneless, skinless chicken breasts
Salt and freshly ground black pepper
2 cups panko
1 tablespoon chopped fresh lemon thyme
1 cup all-purpose flour
4 large eggs, beaten
2 tablespoons extra virgin olive oil
2 cloves garlic, chopped
1 shallot, chopped
1 cup dry sherry
1 cup heavy whipping cream
3/4 cup sour cream
1 heaping teaspoon Dijon mustard
1 heaping teaspoon herb mustard, such as herbes de Provence
2 teaspoons whole-grain mustard

Preheat the oven to 350°F.

Place the chicken breasts on a board and cover with plastic wrap. Using a meat mallet, pound the chicken breasts to even them out and flatten them until they are about 1/2 inch thick. Season well with salt and pepper.

To bread the chicken, combine the panko and lemon thyme in a food processor, and process until the panko is crushed and the mixture is well blended; transfer to a pie plate. Place the flour on a plate and the eggs in a pie plate. Dredge the chicken breasts in the flour, dip them in the egg, then coat well with the panko mixture.

Heat the olive oil in a large sauté pan over medium heat until hot. Add as many chicken breasts as will fit in the pan without overcrowding and fry until golden brown, about 2 minutes per side. Transfer to a sheet pan, and continue with the remaining chicken breasts.

101

(continued)

Pappardelle Tossed with Arugula and Spinach

(continued from page 101)

Place the sheet pan in the oven and bake the chicken just until the breasts are cooked through, about 5 minutes. Transfer to a plate and keep warm.

Meanwhile, to prepare the sauce, remove and discard the panko crumbs from the oil in the sauté pan. Set the pan over high heat and heat until hot. Add the garlic, shallots, and sherry, and reduce until about $1/4$ cup of liquid remains, about 5 minutes. Add the whipping cream and reduce until about $1/2$ cup of liquid remains, about 5 minutes. Add the sour cream and mustards, and mix well. Season to taste with salt and pepper.

To serve, place the chicken on a serving platter and drizzle with some of the sauce. Serve hot, with the remaining sauce on the side.

Cook One:

Pound the chicken breasts.
Bread the chicken.
Brown the chicken, then finish in the oven.
Make the mustard sauce.
Plate and sauce the chicken.

Cook Two:

Prepare the breading station.
Prep the pasta ingredients.
Cook the pappardelle.
Finish the pasta.
Plate the pasta.

Serves 6

1 pound pappardelle
4 ounces soft mild goat cheese
$1/4$ pound fresh baby spinach, rinsed well, spun dry, and stems removed
$1/4$ pound arugula, rinsed well and spun dry
$1/4$ cup extra virgin olive oil
2 cloves garlic, minced
Finely grated zest of 1 lemon
Salt and freshly ground black pepper

Bring a large pot of salted water to a boil. Add the pasta and cook until al dente, about 7 minutes. Just before draining the pasta, ladle out $1/4$ cup of the cooking water and pour it into a large bowl. Drain the pasta well; set aside. Add the goat cheese to the bowl of reserved pasta water and whisk until smooth. Add the greens, olive oil, hot pasta, garlic, and lemon zest, and toss well. Season to taste with salt and pepper. Place on a serving platter. Serve warm.

Menu 31:

Honey-Glazed Grilled Duck

Couscous with Sautéed Cherry
  Tomatoes

Grilled Zucchini with Sweet Soy Sauce

Duck is our favorite poultry to pair with the honey glaze because it is so much more flavorful than chicken. Chicken does make a fine substitute, but keep in mind the cooking time may vary depending on the size of the bird. We like to make couscous when we entertain because it can be served warm, cold, or at room temperature, which takes some of the pressure off the timing of the dishes. Sweet soy sauce, the key element in zucchini marinade, may take a little effort to find. A good-sized Asian grocery store will be your best bet, but if you come up empty-handed, you can use equal parts regular soy sauce sweetened with honey instead. The marinade is so good and easy that you'll want to use it with other summer vegetables, such as eggplant, squash, and artichokes. To complement the sweet flavors of the glaze and the zucchini marinade, we serve a red wine with lots of forward fruit, such as a Barbera or Pinot Noir.

Honey-Glazed Grilled Duck

Serves 6

2 ducklings, about 3 pounds each, split in half
2 teaspoons kosher salt
1/2 teaspoon freshly ground black pepper
1/2 cup dry white wine
2 cloves garlic, minced
1 teaspoon curry powder, toasted (see page 188)
Finely grated zest of 1 lemon
Juice of 1/2 lemon
2/3 cup honey
1 teaspoon soy sauce

To grill the duck, prepare the coals by piling briquettes on one side of the barbecue and lighting them. Let them burn until they are gray in color, about 30 minutes. Remove the grill from the barbecue and oil it well. Season the duck with the salt and pepper, and place it bone-side down on the opposite side of the grill from the coals. Cover the barbecue with the lid, and grill the duck until the thickest place on the thigh reaches an internal temperature of 150°F, about 1 hour.

While the duck is grilling, prepare the glaze. Combine the wine and garlic in a small saucepan over high heat and reduce until about 1/4 cup remains. Add the curry, lemon zest and juice, honey, and soy sauce, and mix well. Set aside.

When the duck is done, move it to the hot side of the grill and baste it very well with the glaze. Grill for about 5 minutes longer, just long enough to caramelize the sauce (be very careful to watch the fire and make sure the duck doesn't burn).

To serve, cut the thighs and legs off the halves and slice the breasts. Arrange the duck on a serving platter or tray, and drizzle with a bit of the remaining glaze. Serve warm.

Couscous with Sautéed Cherry Tomatoes

Serves 6

**3 cups vegetable stock (page 186) or chicken stock
(page 184)**
Salt and freshly ground black pepper
1 1/2 cups couscous
1 tablespoon unsalted butter
2 cups ripe cherry tomatoes
2 cloves garlic, minced
1 shallot, minced
1 tablespoon chopped fresh basil

Heat the stock in a saucepan over high heat until boiling, then season with salt and pepper. In a large bowl, pour the hot stock over the couscous, and cover with aluminum foil. Let stand until the stock is absorbed, about 5 minutes.

Meanwhile, heat the butter in a large sauté pan over high heat until it is melted and bubbling. Add the tomatoes, garlic, and shallot, and sauté just until the tomatoes start to soften, about 3 minutes. Add the basil, toss well, and season to taste with salt and pepper. Transfer the tomatoes to a large bowl.

When the couscous has absorbed all of the stock, fluff it with a fork, add it to the tomato mixture, and mix well. Adjust the seasonings if needed. Serve at room temperature.

Grilled Zucchini with Sweet Soy Sauce

Serves 6

**3 medium zucchini, cut lengthwise into
1/4-inch-thick slices**
1 tablespoon sweet soy sauce
1 clove garlic, minced
1 teaspoon peeled, grated fresh ginger
2 tablespoons vegetable oil
Salt and freshly ground black pepper

Oil the grill and prepare a hot fire. If you are using a gas grill, preheat over high heat. If you are using a charcoal grill, let the coals burn until they are covered with gray ash. The fire is hot when you can hold your hand over the grill for no longer than 5 seconds.

Place the zucchini in a large bowl. In a small bowl, combine the soy sauce, garlic, ginger, and oil, and mix well. Pour the marinade over the zucchini and toss well. Grill the zucchini until crisp-tender, 1 to 2 minutes per side. Season to taste with salt and pepper. Serve warm.

Cook One:

Oil and light the grill.
Make the marinade for the duck.
Make the marinade for the zucchini.
Glaze the duckling and finish it on the hot side of the grill.
Remove the duck from the grill let it rest.
Slice, plate, and sauce the duck.

Cook Two:

Split the duck and season.
Place the duck on the cool side of the grill.
About 15 minutes before the duck is finished, prepare the couscous.
Toss the zucchini with the marinade and grill.
Plate the zucchini and couscous.
Open and pour the wine.

105

Menu 32:

Canard au Vin

Oven-Roasted Carrots

Save this menu for a weekend you want to devote to cooking a hearty feast. In France, the traditional ingredient for this succulent dish is rooster, not duck, but in this country, roosters can be hard to come by in the local market. Duck legs make the best substitute, as they don't dry out when braised. Chicken legs will also work, but don't be tempted to use the breasts—they become tough and dry, defeating all your efforts. The touch of bitter chocolate in the sauce adds a subtle, silky touch and a gorgeous color. To keep the feast true to its roots, a French wine is a must, such as an elegantly complex Bordeaux.

Canard au Vin

Serves 6

6 large bone-in duck legs
4 large carrots, coarsely chopped
4 stalks celery, coarsely chopped
1 large onion, coarsely chopped
6 cloves garlic
1 (750-ml) bottle red wine
2 tablespoons extra virgin olive oil
Salt and freshly ground black pepper
1 cup all-purpose flour
3 cups rich chicken stock (page 184)
1 tablespoon chopped fresh thyme
1 teaspoon chopped fresh marjoram
2 ounces unsweetened chocolate, chopped
6 slices pepper bacon or bacon, diced
1 pound button mushrooms, trimmed
Thyme sprigs, for garnish

Combine the duck legs, carrots, celery, onion, and garlic in a large container, and pour the wine over to cover. Refrigerate for 24 hours.

Preheat the oven to 375°F.

Remove the duck legs from the vegetables and wine (reserve the mixture) and pat dry. Heat the olive oil in a large roasting pan set over two burners on high heat until smoking hot. Season the duck legs with salt and pepper, then dredge in the flour. Brown the duck legs in the oil, 3 to 4 minutes per side. Add the reserved vegetables and wine, bring to a boil, and boil for about 5 minutes. Add the chicken stock, thyme, and marjoram, and bring to a boil. Cover the pan with a lid or foil, set it in the oven, and braise until the legs are tender, about 45 minutes. Remove the pan from the oven. Remove the duck legs from the wine mixture and place on a plate; set aside.

Oven-Roasted Carrots

Serves 6

8 carrots, peeled and cut into large dice
6 cloves garlic, cut into large dice
2 tablespoons extra virgin olive oil
$1/2$ teaspoon freshly ground black pepper
Salt

Preheat the oven to 425°F. Place a sheet pan in the oven to preheat for about 10 minutes.

Combine the carrots, garlic, and olive oil in a bowl, and toss well. Place on the hot sheet pan and roast, stirring only once or twice, until the carrots are tender and brown, about 20 minutes. Add the pepper and season to taste with salt. Place in a serving bowl and serve warm.

Cook One:

Cooks' Note: The duck legs and vegetables for the Canard au Vin must soak in the wine overnight.

Remove the duck legs from the wine, then season and sear.

Finish the braising liquid, and place the duck in the oven.

About 15 minutes before the duck is done, preheat the sheet pan for the carrots.

Roast the carrots.

Plate the carrots.

Cook Two:

Prep the carrots.

While the duck is cooking, make two Manhattans to share with Cook One, and relax.

Remove the duck from the braising liquid and keep warm.

Cook the bacon and mushrooms for the sauce.

Plate, sauce, and garnish the duck.

To prepare the sauce, set the roasting pan back over two burners on high heat, and reduce the wine mixture until it is thick enough to coat the back of a spoon, about 5 minutes. Stir in the chocolate. Decrease the heat to very low and let the sauce simmer for about 3 minutes.

Meanwhile, heat a large sauté pan over medium heat until hot, add the bacon, and cook until very crispy, about 4 minutes. Using a slotted spoon, transfer the bacon to paper towels to drain, reserving the drippings in the pan. Add the mushrooms to the pan and sauté just until the mushrooms are tender, about 5 minutes.

While the mushrooms are cooking, strain the sauce through a fine-mesh sieve into a large sauté pan. Set the pan over medium-high heat. Add the sautéed mushrooms and the bacon drippings, and mix well. Add the duck legs and cook until heated through. Season the sauce to taste with salt and pepper.

To serve, place one duck leg on each plate. Top with the sauce, and garnish with the crispy bacon and thyme sprigs.

107

Menu 33:

Cranberry- and Zinfandel-Brined Turkey

Dried Fruit and Hazelnut Stuffing

Roasted Brussels Sprouts with Bacon

We brine turkeys every Thanksgiving, both at home and in our cooking classes. Brining infuses turkey with flavor and makes it juicy beyond what a typical Thanksgiving bird has to offer. We realize that not everyone has access to a large, restaurant-sized walk-in refrigerator, which might seem necessary when sizing up an 18-pound turkey immersed in almost a gallon of brine, but don't worry. We have a solution for any size kitchen: Line a large cooler with a clean plastic garbage bag, pour in the brine, fully immerse the turkey in the brine, and then seal the bag completely so the brine doesn't leak out. Surround the bag with gel packs to keep the turkey well chilled, replacing them when necessary. No Thanksgiving table is complete without a dozen side dishes, and although we only suggest two here, there are many dishes in this book to grace your holiday table while leaving room for that family favorite.

Cranberry- and Zinfandel-Brined Turkey

Serves 6

BRINE

2 (750-ml) bottles Zinfandel
4 cups apple cider
1 pound fresh cranberries
1 cup honey
1 cup kosher salt
4 sprigs fresh rosemary
1 tablespoon black peppercorns
4 sprigs fresh sage
2 sticks cinnamon

TURKEY

1 (18-pound) turkey, preferably free-range and hormone-free
3 large carrots, coarsely chopped
6 stalks celery, coarsely chopped
3 onions, coarsely chopped

To prepare the brine, combine the wine, cider, cranberries, honey, salt, rosemary, peppercorns, sage, and cinnamon in a large pan over high heat, and bring to a boil. Let the brine boil for about 4 minutes. Remove the pan from the heat, let cool, and refrigerate until it reaches about 40°F. Place the turkey in a very large container, then pour the chilled brine over to cover. Refrigerate for at least 24 hours, or up to 48 hours.

To roast the turkey, preheat the oven to 350°F. Remove the turkey from the brine and drain well (discard the brine). Combine the carrots, celery, and onions in a roasting pan. Set the turkey on top of the vegetables (do not season the turkey with salt and pepper, as the brine has seasoned it). Roast the turkey until reaches an internal temperature of 160°F, tenting it with aluminum foil if it starts to brown too much, about 4 hours.

Let the turkey rest for 5 to 10 minutes before carving. Carve and serve warm.

Dried Fruit and Hazelnut Stuffing

Serves 6

3 tablespoons unsalted butter

1 large onion, diced

3 cloves garlic, chopped

$^1/_2$ cup chopped dried cranberries

$^1/_2$ cup chopped dried pears

$^1/_2$ cup chopped dried apricots

1 cup brandy

$^1/_2$ cup red wine

4 cups diced good-quality bread

3 large eggs, lightly beaten

1 cup chicken stock (page 184) or turkey stock (page 184)

$^3/_4$ cup chopped toasted hazelnuts (see page 188)

2 teaspoons chopped fresh sage

2 teaspoons chopped fresh rosemary

1 tablespoon cayenne sauce

Salt and freshly ground black pepper

Preheat the oven 350°F. Using about 1 tablespoon of the butter, butter a 9 by 13-inch baking dish; set aside.

Heat the remaining 2 tablespoons butter in a large sauté pan over medium heat until melted and bubbling. Add the onion and garlic, and sauté for about 2 minutes. Add the dried fruit and toss well. Remove the pan from the heat, then carefully add the brandy and red wine. Set the pan back on the burner, and reduce over high heat until the mixture is just about dry, 4 to 5 minutes.

Transfer the fruit mixture to a large bowl, and let cool completely. Add the bread and mix well.

Add the eggs to the fruit mixture, and mix well. Add as much of the stock as needed to moisten the stuffing, and mix well. Add the hazelnuts, sage, rosemary, and cayenne sauce. Season well with salt and pepper, and mix well. Transfer the stuffing to the prepared pan, and cover the pan with aluminum foil.

Bake the stuffing for about 40 minutes, then remove the foil and continue baking until the stuffing starts to brown, about 10 minutes longer. Serve warm.

Cook One:

Cooks' Note: The turkey must be brined for at least 24 hours, and not more than 48 hours, before roasting.

Chop the vegetables for the turkey, place in a roasting pan, top with the turkey, and roast.

Prep the ingredients for the Brussels sprouts.

Finish the Brussels sprouts.

Plate the Brussels sprouts and the stuffing.

Cook Two:

Prep the stuffing and refrigerate.

Bake the stuffing.

Remove the turkey from the oven and let rest.

Carve and plate the turkey.

Roasted Brussels Sprouts with Bacon

Serves 6

6 slices bacon, diced
1 large onion, julienned
3 cloves garlic, chopped
2 Granny Smith apples, peeled and cut into large dice
1 ¹/₂ pounds Brussels sprouts, trimmed
2 tablespoons whole-grain mustard
2 tablespoons cider vinegar
2 tablespoons extra virgin olive oil

Preheat the oven to 425°F.

Heat a large ovenproof sauté pan over medium heat until hot. Add the bacon and cook until very crispy, about 4 minutes. Transfer the bacon to paper towels to drain, reserving the drippings in the pan. Add the onion to the pan, and cook, without stirring, until it just begins to brown, about 4 minutes. Add the garlic, apples, and Brussels sprouts, and toss well. Set the pan in the oven and roast the Brussels sprouts just until tender, about 20 minutes.

In a small bowl, whisk together the mustard, vinegar, and oil. Pour the mixture over the Brussels sprouts, add the crispy bacon, and mix well. Season to taste with salt and pepper. Serve warm.

111

Menu 34:

Smoked Balsamic-Glazed Leg of Lamb

Big Fat Oven Fries

Oven-Roasted Asparagus

This simple summer menu does require a bit of forethought and planning, but once the lamb has marinated for 24 hours, the rest of the menu comes together easily. The bone in the leg of lamb helps to keep the meat very moist, and the low cooking temperature assures it remains tender. Roasting asparagus is just about the best way to prepare this tender vegetable. The method is fast and concentrates the flavor, instead of just diluting it like steaming does. We love these big fat oven fries covered in spices, and we especially love how they complement the smokiness of the lamb. This is a great meal for those lazy sunny Sunday afternoons when your only concern is having a great meal, and the best way to top it off is with a full-bodied Pinot Noir.

Smoked Balsamic-Glazed Leg of Lamb

Serves 6

1 bone-in leg of lamb (about 7 pounds)
1 cup John's Secret Cure (page 182)
$^1/_2$ cup high-quality balsamic vinegar (aged at least 10 years)
3 cloves garlic, chopped
$^2/_3$ cup extra virgin olive oil
1 tablespoon freshly ground black pepper
1 tablespoon chopped fresh rosemary
Rosemary sprigs, for garnish

Rub the lamb with the cure and place it in a large non-reactive pan. Fill $^1/_4$ cup of the balsamic vinegar in a food syringe and inject it intermittently into the thickest part of the lamb. Cover the meat and refrigerate it for 24 hours.

To prepare the vinaigrette, whisk together the remaining $^1/_4$ cup vinegar and the garlic in a small bowl. While whisking, slowly add the olive oil and whisk until smooth. Add the pepper and chopped rosemary, and mix well. Set aside.

To smoke the lamb, remove the grill from the barbecue, and then prepare the coals by piling briquettes on one side of the barbecue and lighting them. Let them burn until they are gray in color, about 30 minutes. Place a handful of smoking chips (alder, apple, hickory, or any type of hardwood) on a square of aluminum foil and place the foil on the hot coals. Oil the grill and set it back on the barbecue.

Wipe any excess cure off the lamb with a paper towel, and place the lamb on the opposite side of the grill from the coals. Set an oven thermometer in the barbecue, cover with the lid, and let the lamb smoke until it reaches an internal temperature of 140°F, about 4 hours, basting the lamb with the vinaigrette every hour or so. While the lamb is smoking, add more chips as needed to keep the smoke from dying down, and try to keep the temperature of the barbecue between 250° and 300°F.

(If the temperature gets too high, partially close the air vent to lower the heat, but do not shut the vent completely or else the fire will go out.)

When the lamb is done, remove it from the barbecue and let it sit for about 10 minutes before slicing. Slice thinly, avoiding the bone. To serve, place the lamb slices on a large serving platter and garnish with sprigs of rosemary. Serve hot.

Cook One:

Cooks' Note: The lamb must be cured and marinated overnight.

Oil and light the grill.

Place smoke chips on the grill.

Clean the excess cure off the lamb and place on the grill.

Baste the lamb.

When the lamb reaches the correct internal temperature, remove it from the barbecue and let rest.

Slice, plate, and garnish the lamb.

Open and pour the wine.

Cook Two:

Make the vinaigrette for the asparagus.

Trim the asparagus, place on a sheet pan, and season.

Cut the potatoes, place in a bowl, and cover with water.

Make martinis and share with Cook One while the lamb cooks.

When the lamb is about 30 minutes from being done, preheat the pan for the potatoes.

When the pan is hot, drain the potatoes, season, and roast.

While the lamb is resting, place the prepped asparagus in the oven and roast.

Plate the potatoes and asparagus.

Big Fat Oven Fries

Serves 6

6 large russet potatoes, scrubbed and cut lengthwise into eighths
3 tablespoons extra virgin olive oil
2 teaspoons cumin seeds
2 teaspoons chile powder
2 teaspoons sea salt
1 teaspoon freshly ground black pepper
2 cloves garlic, chopped

Preheat the oven to 425°F.

Set a roasting pan in the oven and heat until very hot, about 10 minutes. Combine the potatoes, oil, cumin, chile powder, salt, and pepper in a large bowl, and toss well. Place the potatoes in a single layer in the hot roasting pan and bake until golden brown, about 15 minutes. Toss and continue baking until tender, about 5 minutes longer. Remove the pan from the oven, add the garlic, and toss well. Serve warm.

Oven-Roasted Asparagus

Serves 6

1 1/2 pounds fresh asparagus, trimmed
2 tablespoons extra virgin olive oil
1 teaspoon sea salt
1/2 teaspoon finely chopped fresh rosemary
1/2 teaspoon freshly ground black pepper

Preheat the oven to 425°F (you will get the best results in a convection oven).

Place the trimmed asparagus in a single layer on a sheet pan. Drizzle with the oil, sprinkle with the sea salt, rosemary, and pepper, and roast until crisp-tender, 4 to 5 minutes, depending on the thickness of the spears. Serve hot.

113

Menu 35:

Slow-Roasted Leg of Lamb with an Herb Jus

Celeriac-Potato Gratin

Sautéed Spinach with Garlic and Zinfandel Wine Vinegar

When we host large dinner parties, we often find ourselves using variations of this menu. It needs so little attention once the main elements go in the oven that we can relax along with our guests. The timing of this menu is a bit different than the others, since the starch takes longer to cook than the entree. The gratin cooks for about an hour, so give it a 40-minute head start before the lamb goes in the oven. The lamb can be incredibly tender if you can roast it at a low temperature and as slowly as possible, but don't go lower than about 225°F. Both the lamb and gratin need time to rest after cooking, which gives you ample time to make the spinach. With this leg of lamb, we serve a lush Merlot with soft round fruit.

Slow-Roasted Leg of Lamb with an Herb Jus

Serves 6

4- to 5-pound boneless leg of lamb, silver skin removed and fat trimmed
2 tablespoons Dijon mustard
1 head garlic, roasted (see page 187)
8 shallots, roasted (see page 188)
1 teaspoon chopped fresh rosemary
Salt and freshly ground black pepper
1 tablespoon extra virgin olive oil

HERB JUS
1 cup red wine
2 cloves garlic, chopped
1 shallot, chopped
6 cups chicken stock (page 184)
1 teaspoon chopped fresh thyme
1 teaspoon chopped fresh basil
1 teaspoon chopped fresh rosemary
Salt and freshly ground black pepper

Rosemary sprigs, for garnish

Preheat the oven to 300°F.

To prepare the lamb, place it on a board and cover with plastic wrap. Using a meat mallet, pound the lamb to even it out. Spread the mustard over one side of the meat. Combine the garlic, shallots, and chopped rosemary in a food processor and process until smooth. Spread the shallot mixture over the mustard. Roll the meat jelly-roll style and secure with butcher's twine. Season well with salt and pepper.

Heat the oil in a large ovenproof sauté pan over high heat until smoking hot. Add the lamb and sear well, about 5 minutes per side. Set the pan in the oven and roast the lamb until it reaches an internal temperature of 135°F, about 1 hour.

Remove the lamb from the pan, and transfer it to a sheet pan. Cover with aluminum foil and let rest. Remove and discard as much of the fat as possible from the drippings in the pan; reserve the drippings in the pan.

While the lamb is roasting, prepare the herb jus. Combine the wine, garlic, and shallot in a saucepan over high heat and reduce until about $1/2$ cup remains, about 5 minutes. Add the stock and reduce until about 2 cups of liquid remain, about 15 minutes. Add the thyme, basil, and rosemary. Decrease the heat to low, and simmer until the lamb is ready.

Set the sauté pan with the reserved drippings over high heat. Add the herb jus and cook, stirring often, to deglaze the pan. Season to taste with salt and pepper; keep warm.

To serve, slice the lamb and place it on a serving platter. Garnish with rosemary sprigs. Serve warm, with the herb jus on the side.

Celeriac-Potato Gratin

Serves 6

3 large celeriac, peeled and thinly sliced
Salt and freshly ground black pepper
1 $1/2$ cups heavy whipping cream
1 cup grated Swiss cheese
1 cup freshly grated good-quality Parmesan cheese
3 large Yukon Gold potatoes, peeled and thinly sliced
2 tablespoons chopped fresh thyme

Preheat the oven to 350°F. Lightly grease a 9 by 13-inch baking dish.

Arrange about half of the celeriac slices in the bottom of the pan to evenly cover, then season with salt and pepper. Drizzle with about $1/2$ cup of the cream, and top with $1/3$ cup of each of the cheeses. Arrange the potato slices to evenly cover the cheese, then season with salt and pepper. Drizzle with about $1/2$ cup of the cream, and top with $1/3$ cup of each of the cheeses. Repeat with the remaining celeriac, cream, and cheeses. Sprinkle with the thyme. Bake for about 1 hour, until tender. Let rest for 3 to 5 minutes, then cut into serving pieces. Serve warm.

Sautéed Spinach with Garlic and Zinfandel Wine Vinegar

Serves 6

2 tablespoons unsalted butter

2 cloves garlic, chopped

2 bunches spinach (about $^3/_4$ pound), rinsed well, spun dry, and stems removed

2 tablespoons Zinfandel wine vinegar

1 teaspoon soy sauce

Freshly ground black pepper

Heat the butter in a large sauté pan over medium heat until melted and bubbling. Add the garlic and sauté for about 2 minutes. Add the spinach and cook just until it starts to wilt, about 30 seconds. Add the vinegar and soy sauce, and cook just until the spinach is just tender, about 2 minutes. Season to taste with pepper. Serve warm.

Cook One:

Roast the shallots and garlic.

Trim the lamb, then pound to even out the meat.

Make the lamb stuffing.

Start the reduction for the lamb jus.

Stuff the leg of lamb and sear, then place in the oven.

When the lamb reaches the correct internal temperature, remove it from the oven and let it rest.

Slice, plate, and garnish the lamb.

Cut and plate the gratin.

Cook Two:

Peel and slice the potatoes and celeriac.

Make the gratin and place in the oven.

Prep the ingredients for the spinach dish.

Add the stock to the herb jus reduction and simmer.

Finish preparing the herb jus and pour it into a sauce boat.

Cook the spinach.

Plate the spinach.

Open and pour the wine.

Rack of Lamb with Merlot Glaze and Cherry Reduction Sauce

Sea Salt–Roasted Creamers

Lemon Green Beans

Neither of us has a favorite dish per se, but we do have a favorite meat—rack of lamb. When we want to prepare a truly special dinner, we often use rack of lamb as the focal point. This menu really shows it off, although it is a bit labor-intensive. When faced with a challenging menu like this one, working with a partner in the kitchen makes all the difference. In case you are unfamiliar with creamers, they are golf ball–sized potatoes with a delicate white skin and creamy flesh; they are generally available in farmers' markets and gourmet grocery stores. A full-bodied Merlot or other red wine with intense berry flavors makes a lovely complement.

Rack of Lamb with a Merlot Glaze and Cherry Reduction Sauce

Serves 6

CHERRY REDUCTION SAUCE

2 cups Merlot or other red wine
2 cups fresh cherries, pitted
2 cloves garlic, chopped
1 shallot, chopped
4 cups lamb stock (page 185) or chicken stock (page 184)
1 tablespoon unsalted butter
Salt and freshly ground black pepper

MERLOT GLAZE

1 (750-ml) bottle Merlot
1 1/2 cups good-quality balsamic vinegar (aged at least 5 years)
1 shallot, chopped
1 clove garlic, chopped

LAMB

4 racks lamb, 1 1/2 to 2 pounds each, excess fat trimmed and bones frenched (see page 188)
Salt and freshly ground black pepper
1 tablespoon extra virgin olive oil

Fresh cherries, for garnish
Rosemary sprigs, for garnish

To prepare the sauce, combine the wine, cherries, garlic, and shallot in a saucepan over high heat and reduce until the mixture is almost dry, about 10 minutes. Add the stock, decrease the heat to medium, and reduce until the sauce is thick and coats the back of a spoon, 10 to 15 minutes. Add the butter and stir until melted. Season to taste with salt and pepper. Keep warm until you are ready to serve.

Preheat the oven to 300°F.

To prepare the glaze, combine the wine, vinegar, shallot, and garlic in a saucepan over medium heat and reduce until about 1/2 cup of liquid remains, 20 to 25 minutes. Set aside until you are ready to use it.

To prepare the lamb, season the racks well with salt and pepper. Heat the olive oil in a large sauté pan over high heat until smoking hot. Add as many of the racks as will fit without overcrowding the pan, meat side down, and sear well, 3 to 4 minutes; transfer to a sheet pan. Continue searing the remaining racks. Baste the racks well with the glaze. Set the pan in the oven and roast, basting every 5 minutes, until the meat reaches an internal temperature of 135°F for medium-rare doneness about 20 minutes. Remove the racks from the oven and let sit for about 5 minutes, then slice.

(continued)

(continued from page 117)

To serve, place the slices on a serving platter and drizzle with some of the sauce. Garnish with cherries and rosemary sprigs. Serve warm, with any extra sauce on the side.

Cook One:

Start the reduction for the sauce.

Blanch and shock the green beans.

Sear the lamb and place on a sheet pan.

Turn the oven temperature down and place the lamb in the oven.

Baste the lamb.

Remove the lamb from the oven and let rest.

Slice, plate, and garnish the lamb.

Cook Two:

Start the reduction for the glaze.

Add the stock to the sauce.

Preheat a roasting pan and roast the potatoes.

Remove the potatoes from the oven and keep warm.

Cook the green beans.

Plate and garnish the green beans and the potatoes.

Open and serve the wine.

Sea Salt–Roasted Creamers

Serves 6

3 pounds creamer potatoes, scrubbed
2 tablespoons extra virgin olive oil
1 tablespoon sea salt
2 teaspoons chopped fresh rosemary
2 cloves garlic, minced
Freshly ground black pepper

Preheat the oven to 400°F.

Place a roasting pan in the oven to preheat for about 10 minutes. In a large bowl, combine the potatoes and olive oil, and toss well.

When the roasting pan is hot, add the potatoes and 1 teaspoon of the salt and shake the pan to stir. Roast the potatoes for about 10 minutes, add another teaspoon of the salt and shake. Continue roasting until the potatoes are tender, 10 to 15 minutes longer.

Remove the pan from the oven, add the remaining 1 teaspoon salt, rosemary, and garlic. Shake the pan to stir, then season to taste with pepper. Keep the potatoes warm until you are ready to serve.

Lemon Green Beans

Serves 6

2 tablespoons unsalted butter
1 pound fresh green beans, trimmed, blanched,
    and shocked (see page 188)
2 cloves garlic, minced
Juice and finely grated zest of 1 lemon
Salt and freshly ground black pepper

119

Heat the butter in a large sauté pan until it is bubbling and slightly brown. Add the green beans, garlic, and lemon juice and zest, and toss well. Cook just until the beans are warm, about 3 minutes. Season to taste with salt and pepper. Serve warm.

Menu 37:

Marinated Lamb Kebabs with Chile-Yogurt Sauce

Couscous with Spiced Almonds

Red Onion and Cucumber Salad

This is a menu you'll want to pull out when you entertain on those really hot evenings. Much of the prep work can be done early in the day when it's cooler, so all you'll have left to do is grill the kebabs and pour the stock over the couscous. With so little cooking indoors, your kitchen will never heat up. For a spicy-hot evening of Mediterranean delights enjoyed outside in a star-filled night, offer ice-cold beer or a well-chilled champagne.

Marinated Lamb Kebabs with Chile-Yogurt Sauce

Serves 6

2 1/2 pounds lamb shoulder, cut into 1-inch cubes
1 sweet onion, such as a Walla Walla, diced
2 cloves garlic, chopped
Finely grated zest of 1 orange
Juice of 3 oranges
2 tablespoons chopped fresh mint
1/4 cup extra virgin olive oil
Salt and freshly ground black pepper

Mint sprigs, for garnish

CHILE-YOGURT SAUCE
1 cup whole-milk yogurt
2 cloves garlic, minced
2 teaspoons cumin, toasted (see page 188)
1 tablespoon chile powder, toasted (see page 188)
Salt and freshly ground black pepper

To prepare the kebabs, skewer the lamb pieces alternating with the onions onto six large metal skewers. Place the kebabs in a large baking dish. In a small bowl, whisk together the garlic, orange zest and juice, mint, and oil. Pour the marinade over the kebabs and refrigerate for at least 30 minutes, or up to 2 hours.

While the lamb is marinating, prepare the yogurt sauce. Whisk together the yogurt, garlic, cumin, and chile powder in a bowl. Season to taste with salt and pepper. Refrigerate until you are ready to serve.

To grill the kebabs, oil the grill and prepare a hot fire. If you are using a gas grill, preheat on high. If you are using a charcoal grill, let the coals burn until they are covered with gray ash. The fire is hot when you can hold your hand over the grill for no longer than 5 seconds. Remove the lamb from the marinade and drain very well. Place the skewers on the grill and grill, turning once or twice, for 6 to 8 minutes for medium doneness.

Place the skewers on a serving platter, and garnish with mint sprigs. Serve warm, with the sauce on the side.

Couscous with Spiced Almonds

Serves 6

SPICED ALMONDS

2 tablespoons unsalted butter

1 cup whole blanched almonds

1 teaspoon ground cumin

$1/4$ teaspoon ground turmeric

$1/2$ teaspoon ground coriander

$1/2$ teaspoon sweet paprika

1 teaspoon sea salt

COUSCOUS

3 cups chicken stock (page 184) or vegetable stock (page 186)

Salt and freshly ground black pepper

1 $1/2$ cups couscous

To prepare the almonds, heat the butter in a sauté pan over medium heat until it is melted and bubbling. Add the almonds, cumin, turmeric, coriander, paprika, and salt. Sauté until the almonds start to brown and the spices smell very fragrant, 4 to 5 minutes. Let cool.

To prepare the couscous, heat the stock in a saucepan over high heat until boiling, then season with salt and pepper. Place the couscous in a large bowl, pour the hot stock over the couscous, and cover with foil. Let stand until the stock is absorbed, about 5 minutes.

Meanwhile, coarsely chop the cooled almonds. When the couscous has absorbed the stock, fluff with a fork, add the almonds, and mix well. Season to taste with salt and pepper. Serve warm or at room temperature.

Red Onion and Cucumber Salad

Serves 6

2 red onions, julienned
Salt
3 English cucumbers, peeled, seeded, and thinly sliced
2 teaspoons peeled, grated fresh ginger
2 cloves garlic, minced
2 tablespoons minced fresh chives
2 tablespoons rice vinegar
$1/4$ cup vegetable oil, preferably canola
Pinch of crushed red pepper flakes
Freshly ground black pepper

Place the onions in a large bowl; set aside.

In a colander, lightly salt the cucumbers and let drain for about 10 minutes.

Meanwhile, whisk together the ginger, garlic, chives, and vinegar in a small bowl. While whisking, slowly add the oil and whisk until smooth. Add the pepper flakes, and season to taste with salt and pepper.

Add the cucumbers to the onions, and toss well. Add the dressing and toss well. Adjust the seasonings. Refrigerate for at least 30 minutes, or up to 24 hours, before serving. Serve chilled.

Cook One:

Slice the red onions and salt the cucumbers.
Finish preparing the cucumber salad and refrigerate.
Oil and light the grill.
Make the spiced almonds.
Make the couscous.
Plate the cucumber salad and the couscous.

Cook Two:

Dice the lamb and the onions.
Skewer the lamb and onions.
Make the marinade, then marinate the skewers.
Make the yogurt sauce and refrigerate.
Grill the kebabs
Plate and garnish the kebabs, with sauce on the side.

Menu 38:

Roasted Pork Loin with Calvados and Ginger Sauce

Mashed Potatoes with Caramelized Apples

Seared Cauliflower with Brown Butter

We always strive to create menus with flavors that complement or play off each other, but when we first prepared this one, we were especially thrilled with how well the dishes worked together. From the apple-flavored Calvados in the sauce and the crispy bits of apple in the potatoes to the nutty brown butter in the cauliflower, each element builds upon the other in a delicious symphony. To ensure your dinner doesn't hit a flat note, be sure to keep from overcooking the pork. Take it out of the oven when it reaches an internal temperature of no more than 140°F. As it rests, the temperature will come up an additional 5 to 7 degrees, ensuring that the pork will be moist and perfectly cooked. For the potatoes, contrast is the key, so use a firm, tart baking apple that will stand apart from the creamy potatoes. When choosing a wine, we suggest a lighter-style Pinot Noir that won't overwhelm the delicate flavors of the pork.

Roasted Pork Loin with Calvados and Ginger Sauce

Serves 6

3-pound boneless pork loin
Salt and freshly ground black pepper
2 tablespoons extra virgin olive oil
4 shallots, quartered
6 cloves garlic
1 tablespoon peeled, chopped fresh ginger
3/4 cup Calvados
1/2 cup good-quality apple cider
1 cup chicken stock (page 184)
1 1/2 cups heavy whipping cream

Preheat the oven to 300°F.

Season the pork loin well with salt and pepper. Heat the oil in a roasting pan set over high heat until smoking hot. Add the pork and sear well, about 3 minutes per side. Add the shallots, garlic, and ginger, and sauté for about 1 minute. Set the pan in the oven and roast the pork until it reaches an internal temperature of 140°F for medium doneness, about 40 minutes. Remove the pan from the oven, transfer the pork to a sheet pan, and cover with foil. Set aside while you make the sauce.

To prepare the sauce, set the roasting pan on top of the stove with the burners off, and add the Calvados and cider. Turn the burners on high and let the cider and Calvados reduce until about 1/4 cup of liquid remains. Add the stock and bring to a boil, then add the cream and bring to a boil again. Season to taste with salt and pepper. Strain the sauce through a fine sieve, pressing on the vegetables to help release all the liquid.

To serve, slice the pork and place it on a serving platter. Serve hot, with the sauce on the side.

Mashed Potatoes with Caramelized Apples

Serves 4

2 pounds Yukon Gold potatoes, peeled and diced
2/3 cup heavy whipping cream
2 tablespoons unsalted butter
Salt and freshly ground black pepper
1 tablespoon extra virgin olive oil
2 Granny Smith apples, peeled and diced
1 clove garlic, minced

Preheat the oven to 350°F.

In a large saucepan, add enough cold water to cover the potatoes. Bring to a boil and cook over medium heat until very tender, about 10 minutes. Drain well. Arrange the potatoes in a single layer on a sheet pan, and bake for about 10 minutes to dry. Rice or mash the potatoes in a large bowl; set aside.

Heat the cream and butter in a saucepan over high heat just until the cream comes to a boil. Pour over the potatoes and mix well. Season to taste with salt and pepper. Cover and set aside.

Heat the oil in a sauté pan over high heat until smoking hot. Add the apples and cook, without stirring, until brown, about 3 minutes. Toss and cook until golden brown, about 3 minutes longer. Remove the pan from the heat, add the garlic, and toss well. Fold the apples into the mashed potatoes. Serve warm.

Seared Cauliflower with Brown Butter

Serves 6

1 large head cauliflower, cut into 6 wedges
2 teaspoons extra virgin olive oil
4 tablespoons unsalted butter
1 clove garlic, minced
1 teaspoon white wine vinegar
1 tablespoon chopped fresh tarragon
Sea salt and freshly ground black pepper

In a large pan over high heat, bring about 8 cups of salted water to a boil. Add the cauliflower and cook until crisp-tender, 4 to 5 minutes; drain well. Heat the oil in a large sauté pan over high heat until smoking hot. Add the drained cauliflower and sear until brown, 2 to 3 minutes per side. Transfer to a serving platter or tray and set aside.

Heat the butter in a small sauté pan over high heat until melted and bubbling, and continue cooking until golden brown, about 1 minute. Add the garlic, vinegar, and tarragon, and mix well. Season to taste with salt and pepper. Pour the brown butter over the cauliflower. Serve warm.

Cook One:

Season and sear the pork loin, then place in the oven.
Blanch the cauliflower.
When the pork reaches the correct internal temperature, remove it from the oven, cover, and let rest.
Finish preparing the cauliflower.
Slice and plate the pork.

Cook Two:

Peel the potatoes and put on to cook.
Finish preparing the mashed potatoes.
Make the sauce for the pork and pour it into a sauce boat.
Plate the cauliflower and the mashed potatoes.
Open and pour the wine.

Menu 39:

Pork Short Ribs Braised in Curry with Apples and Chiles

Sautéed Baby Bok Choy with
Basil and Cilantro

Steamed Sticky Rice

Spicy braised short ribs is one of the best dishes you can serve to warm up a cold night. You can substitute beef short ribs for the pork if you like, but you will need to adjust the cooking time depending on their size. As with most things that are braised, the ribs will be even better the next day, so if you have the time, you can prepare and just undercook them in advance, let them cool in the braising liquid, and then finish cooking them just before serving. We like to serve a very dry Gewürztraminer with this menu, since the spicy nature of the grape makes it a natural choice for the spices in the recipes.

Pork Short Ribs Braised in Curry with Apples and Chiles

Serves 6

4 pounds bone-in pork short ribs
Salt and freshly ground black pepper
2 tablespoons vegetable oil
1 large onion, minced
3 cloves garlic, chopped
2 tablespoons peeled, grated fresh ginger
2 tablespoons curry powder
1 cup dry white wine
1 cup good-quality apple cider
4 cups chicken stock (page 184)
$^1/_2$ cup diced dried apples
4 Anaheim chiles, roasted, peeled, seeded (see page 187), and diced
$^1/_4$ cup cilantro leaves, for garnish

Preheat the oven to 375°F.

Season the ribs with salt and pepper. Heat the oil in a large roasting pan set over high heat until smoking hot. Add the ribs and sear well, about 2 minutes per side. Add the onion, garlic, and ginger, and sauté for about 2 minutes. Add the curry powder and sauté for about 1 minute. Add the wine and cider, and reduce until about $^1/_2$ cup of liquid remains, about 5 minutes. Add the stock, apples, and chiles, and bring to a boil. Cover the pan with a lid or foil, set it in the oven, and cook the ribs for 40 to 50 minutes, until tender.

Remove the pan from the oven. Remove the ribs from the sauce and transfer to a plate; set aside. Skim as much of the fat as possible from the sauce. Set the pan with the sauce over high heat and reduce for about 5 minutes. Season to taste with salt and pepper.

To serve, place the ribs on a serving platter and pour the warm sauce over the top. Serve warm, garnished with cilantro leaves.

Sautéed Baby Bok Choy with Basil and Cilantro

Serves 6

1 tablespoon peeled, grated fresh ginger
2 cloves garlic, minced
$^1/_2$ cup mirin
1 tablespoon minced fresh basil
2 teaspoons minced fresh cilantro
2 tablespoons rice vinegar
$^1/_2$ teaspoon Asian chile paste
1 tablespoon vegetable oil
6 baby bok choy, halved lengthwise
Soy sauce

In a small bowl, whisk together the ginger, garlic, mirin, basil, cilantro, vinegar, and chile paste; set aside.

Heat the oil in a large sauté pan over high heat until smoking hot. Add the bok choy and sauté for about 2 minutes. Add the sauce and sauté until tender, 2 to 3 minutes. Season to taste with soy sauce. Place the bok choy on a serving platter. Serve warm.

Steamed Sticky Rice

Serves 6

2 $^1/_2$ cups sticky or sweet rice
1 $^1/_2$ cups cold water
$^3/_4$ teaspoon salt

In a bowl, combine the rice with enough warm water to cover, and let sit for 1 hour. Drain the rice well and place in a metal mixing bowl. Add the cold water and the salt, and cover the bowl with foil or a lid. Set the bowl over a pan of simmering water and cook, adding more water to the bottom pan as needed, until the rice is tender and has absorbed all of the water, about 45 minutes. Place the rice in a serving bowl, and serve warm.

Cook One:

Soak the rice.

Prep the onion, garlic, and ginger for the ribs.

Season and sear the ribs.

Finish preparing the braising liquid, and place the ribs in the oven.

Make the sauce for the bok choy.

Remove the ribs from the oven, and season the braising liquid.

Plate and garnish the ribs.

Cook Two:

Roast the chiles.

Peel, seed, and dice the chiles.

Clean the bok choy.

Cook the rice.

When the rice and pork are just finishing, cook the bok choy.

Plate the rice and the bok choy.

Open and serve the wine.

Menu 40:

John's Ribs with Plum Barbecue Sauce

Sautéed Baby Mustard Greens

Curry Rice Salad

Sometimes we just don't have a say in choosing the menu for our own party. When we phone our friends to invite them for a casual gathering, more often than not the response is, "You are making ribs, aren't you?" And with that, our dreams of branching out diminish with each call. There's no denying that his ribs are something to look forward to, so John gladly grants their wishes. This means that with every batch of ribs he dutifully prepares, his creative outlet becomes the sauce. The plums and cherry soda give this rendition a jammy-sweet quality that highlights the sauce's Asian elements and melds with the curried salad. In honor of John's southern roots, we often serve a classic side of greens—but instead of stewing them, we like to give them a quick sauté to retain their peppery bite.

John's Ribs with Plum Barbecue Sauce

Serves 6

PLUM BARBECUE SAUCE
2 tablespoons extra virgin olive oil
1 onion, diced
2 stalks celery, diced
4 cloves garlic, chopped
6 fresh plums, diced
2 tablespoons peeled, grated fresh ginger
1 (12 ounce) bottle cherry soda
1 cup dry white wine
1 cup chicken stock (page 184)
1/2 cup ketchup
1/4 cup hoisin sauce
1/4 cup tamarind concentrate
1 tablespoon chile powder
1 tablespoon ground cumin
1 tablespoon smoked paprika
1 tablespoon dry mustard
1 tablespoon plum vinegar or
    red wine vinegar
1 teaspoon canned chipotle chile in adobo sauce
1 bay leaf
Salt

5 pounds pork ribs, preferably St. Louis style or spare ribs, membrane removed
Salt and freshly ground black pepper

To prepare the sauce, heat the olive oil in a large sauté pan over high heat until very hot. Add the onions, celery, and garlic, and sauté for about 3 minutes. Add the plums and ginger, and sauté until the plums start to soften, 2 to 3 minutes. Add the soda, wine, stock, ketchup, hoisin sauce, tamarind, chile powder, cumin, paprika, mustard, vinegar, chipotle, and bay leaf. Decrease the heat to medium and simmer the sauce for at least 30 minutes, or up to an hour if possible. Transfer the sauce to a blender and purée until smooth. Season to taste with salt. Refrigerate the sauce until you are ready to use it. (The sauce will keep refrigerated for up to 3 weeks.)

129

(continued)

(continued from page 129)

To prepare the ribs, remove the grill from the barbecue, and then prepare the coals by piling briquettes on one side of the barbecue and lighting them. Let them burn until they are gray in color, about 30 minutes. Place a handful of smoking chips (alder, apple, hickory, or any type of hardwood) in a square of foil and place the foil on the hot coals. Oil the grill and set it back on the barbecue. Season the ribs with salt and pepper, place them on the opposite side of the grill from the coals, and cover the grill with the lid. Let the ribs cook for about 45 minutes, then brush with the plum sauce. Cover and continue cooking, brushing the ribs with the sauce every 45 minutes or so and turning them over after about 2 hours, until tender, about 4 hours. While the ribs are cooking, add more coals and chips as needed to keep the smoke from dying down. When the ribs are tender, move them to the hot side of the grill, brush them with the sauce one last time, and cook just until the sauce starts to caramelize, about 5 minutes.

Cut the ribs into two-rib segments. Serve warm with extra sauce on the side.

Sautéed Baby Mustard Greens

Serves 6

1 tablespoon extra virgin olive oil
2 cloves garlic, chopped
2 pounds baby mustard greens, rinsed well and spun dry
2 tablespoons malt vinegar
2 tablespoons unsalted butter
Salt and freshly ground black pepper

Heat the olive oil in a large sauté pan over high heat until hot. Add the garlic and sauté for about 1 minute. Add the mustard greens, vinegar, and butter, cover the pan with a lid, and cook just until the greens are just wilted, about 3 minutes. Remove the pan from the heat, then season to taste with salt and pepper. Transfer to a serving platter and serve warm.

Curry Rice Salad

Serves 6

2 cups cooked basmati rice (page 183)
1 red onion, julienned
4 scallions, both white and green parts, sliced
$^1/_2$ cup sliced water chestnuts
$^1/_4$ cup julienned fresh basil
$^1/_4$ cup julienned fresh mint
2 cloves garlic, chopped
1 tablespoon peeled, grated fresh ginger
$^1/_4$ cup seasoned rice vinegar
1 tablespoon curry powder, toasted (see page 188)
Finely grated zest of 2 limes
2 teaspoons Tom Yum Instant Hot and Sour Paste (optional)
$^2/_3$ cup vegetable oil, preferably canola
Soy sauce

Place the rice in a large bowl. Add the red onion, scallions, water chestnuts, basil, and mint, and mix well; set aside.

To prepare the dressing, whisk together the garlic, ginger, vinegar, curry powder, lime zest, and instant hot and sour paste in a large bowl. While whisking, slowly add the oil and whisk until smooth. Season to taste with soy sauce.

Pour the dressing over the rice mixture and toss well. Refrigerate for at least 30 minutes before serving. Serve chilled.

Cook One:

Make the barbecue sauce.

Grill the ribs.

Open two ice-cold beers to share with Cook Two while the ribs are cooking.

Finish the rice salad.

Slice and plate the ribs.

Cook Two:

Oil and light the grill.

Baste the ribs with the sauce every 45 minutes or so.

Prepare the salad and the dressing.

Just as the ribs are finished cooking, cook the mustard greens.

Plate the rice salad and the mustard greens.

Menu 41:

Grilled Pork Tenderloin with Tahini Marinade

Tabbouleh

Herb-Grilled Eggplant

Years ago, when we were first married and living in Seattle, one of our favorite inexpensive places to eat was a little hole-in-the-wall called the Mediterranean Kitchen. We always ordered one particular dish, chicken wings marinated in a tahini sauce, and as much as we would try to branch out with other items on the menu, we always came back for the crispy, garlicky chicken wings. Moving to Portland several years later meant that we had to come up with our own version of the sauce to satisfy our craving. Thinking we could never improve on those chicken wings, we began slathering the marinade on other things, trying everything from whole chickens to New York steak. An abundance of tahini-enhanced meals later, we were surprised when we finally tasted a combination even better than what lives in our memory, and this current menu evolved. With the nutty, garlicky marinade on pork tenderloin, we serve a lemony tabbouleh with lots of fresh herbs to cleanse the palate and bring a refreshing note to the meal. Although simply grilled, once on the plate, the eggplant soaks up the flavors of the pork and the salad, making it even more wonderful.

Grilled Pork Tenderloin with Tahini Marinade

Serves 6

$1/4$ cup tahini paste
3 cloves garlic, minced
Juice and finely grated zest of 2 lemons
$1/4$ cup extra virgin olive oil, plus more for drizzling
2 teaspoons groound cumin
2 teaspoons smoked paprika
1 teaspoon Asian chile paste
2 $1/2$ pounds pork tenderloin, trimmed
Salt and freshly ground black pepper

To prepare the marinade, combine the tahini paste, garlic, lemon juice and zest, oil, cumin, paprika, and chile paste in a food processor and process until smooth. Coat the tenderloin with the marinade, place in a large baking dish, and refrigerate for about 30 minutes to marinate.

Meanwhile, oil the grill and prepare a hot fire. If you are using a gas grill, preheat on high. If you are using a charcoal grill, let the coals burn until they are covered with gray ash. The fire is hot when you can hold your hand over the grill for no longer than 5 seconds.

Remove the tenderloin from the marinade (discard the marinade), and season well with salt and pepper. Place the tenderloin on the grill and grill for 4 to 6 minutes per side for medium-rare doneness. Let the meat rest for 3 to 5 minutes.

Thinly slice the meat at an angle. Place the slices on a serving platter, and drizzle with a bit of extra virgin olive oil. Serve warm.

Tabbouleh

Serves 6

1 cup finely ground bulghur wheat
1 cup water, at room temperature
$^1/_4$ cup chopped flat-leaf parsley
$^1/_4$ cup chopped fresh mint
2 tablespoons chopped fresh cilantro
4 scallions, both white and green parts, chopped
2 red bell peppers, roasted, peeled, seeded (see page 188), and diced
3 cloves garlic, chopped
$^1/_2$ cup freshly squeezed lemon juice
Finely grated zest of 2 lemons
$^1/_3$ cup extra virgin olive oil
1 teaspoon Asian chile paste
Salt and freshly ground black pepper

In a large bowl, combine the bulghur and water, and let sit until all of the water is absorbed, 15 to 20 minutes. Add the parsley, mint, cilantro, scallions, and bell peppers, and toss well.

Whisk together the garlic, lemon juice and zest, oil, and chile paste in a bowl. Pour the dressing over the salad and mix well. Season to taste with salt and pepper.

Let the salad sit at room temperature for about 30 minutes before serving, or refrigerate for up to 24 hours. Serve at room temperature or chilled.

Cook One:

Make the pork marinade and marinate.
Oil and light the grill.
Chop the herbs.
Grill the pork and the eggplant.
Slice and plate the pork

Herb-Grilled Eggplant

Serves 6

2 eggplants, cut horizontally into $^1/_2$-inch-thick rounds
Juice and finely grated zest of 2 lemons
$^1/_4$ cup extra virgin olive oil
1 tablespoon cumin seeds
2 teaspoons fennel seeds
2 tablespoons chopped fresh oregano
1 tablespoon chopped fresh flat-leaf parsley
Salt and freshly ground black pepper
Oregano or flat-leaf parsley sprigs, for garnish

Place the eggplant slices in a large bowl; set aside. In a small bowl, whisk together the lemon juice and zest and the oil. In a small sauté pan over high heat, toast the cumin and fennel seeds for about 1 minute, and grind until a fine powder. Add the ground spices and the oregano and parsley to the lemon juice mixture, and mix well. Pour the marinade over the eggplant, toss to coat, and marinate at room temperature for about 30 minutes.

Meanwhile, oil the grill and prepare a hot fire. If you are using a gas grill, preheat on high. If you are using a charcoal grill, let the coals burn until they are covered with gray ash. The fire is hot when you can hold your hand over the grill for no longer than 5 seconds.

Drain the eggplant well, and season with salt and pepper. Place the eggplant on the grill and grill until brown, about 3 minutes per side.

To serve, place the eggplant on a serving platter and garnish with sprigs of oregano. Serve warm.

133

Cook Two:

Make the eggplant marinade and marinate.
Soak the bulghur wheat for the tabbouleh.
Finish the tabbouleh.
Plate the tabbouleh and the eggplant.

Menu 42:

Ginger-Glazed Stuffed Pork Chops
Briased Belgian Endives

We always try to find ways to streamline the cooking when we're entertaining, even though we're working together in the kitchen. One of the ways we do this is by combining the entrée with one or both of the side dishes, and this menu provides a perfect example. As the pork chops bake, they baste the hearty side dish sandwiched within, a moist cornbread stuffing sweetened with bits of dried apricot. All that's left to tackle is a classic vegetable dish to round out the menu. The world's most versatile food wine, Pinot Noir, keeps the dinner on course.

Ginger-Glazed Stuffed Pork Chops

Serves 6

CORNBREAD -APRICOT STUFFING
1 tablespoon extra virgin olive oil
1 small onion, finely diced
2 cloves garlic, chopped
$^1/_2$ cup diced dried apricots
$^3/_4$ cup dry sherry
3 cups diced cornbread (page 181)
1 large egg, lightly beaten
$^1/_2$ cup chicken stock (page 184)
1 tablespoon chopped fresh flat-leaf parsley
Salt and freshly ground black pepper

6 (10-ounce) double-thick pork chops
Salt and freshly ground black pepper
1 tablespoon extra virgin olive oil

GINGER GLAZE
1 cup dry sherry
1 tablespoon peeled, grated fresh ginger
1 clove garlic, chopped
$^1/_2$ cup chicken stock (page 184)
2 tablespoons honey
1 tablespoon freshly squeezed lemon juice
2 teaspoons soy sauce
Dash of Asian chile sauce

Preheat the oven to 425°F.

To prepare the stuffing, heat the olive oil in a large sauté pan over high heat until very hot. Add the onion and garlic, and sauté for 2 to 3 minutes. Add the apricots and sherry, and cook until the mixture is almost dry, about 5 minutes. Remove the pan from the heat. Transfer the apricot mixture to a large bowl, and let cool completely. Add the cornbread and egg to the cooled apricot mixture, and mix well. Add enough of the stock to moisten the stuffing. Add the parsley, season with salt and pepper, and mix well.

Braised Belgian Endives

Serves 6

1 tablespoon extra virgin olive oil
6 large Belgian endives, halved
2 cloves garlic, chopped
$^1/_2$ cup dry sherry
1 tablespoon sherry vinegar
$^1/_4$ cup vegetable stock (page 186)
2 teaspoons Dijon mustard
1 tablespoon unsalted butter
Salt and freshly ground black pepper

To prepare the pork chops, cut a 1-inch slit in the side of each chop and open to form a pocket. Place the stuffing in a pastry bag without a tip, place the end of the pastry bag in the pocket of one of the chops, and squeeze to fill the chop with stuffing. Continue with the remaining chops and stuffing. Season the pork chops with salt and pepper.

Heat the oil in a large ovenproof sauté pan over high heat until smoking hot. Add the pork chops and sear well, 3 to 4 minutes per side. Set the pan in the oven and roast the chops for about 20 minutes, until cooked through.

To prepare the glaze, transfer the chops to a serving platter and keep warm, reserving the drippings in the pan. Place the pan on a burner, add the sherry, ginger, and garlic, and reduce over high heat until about $^1/_4$ cup of liquid remains, about 4 minutes. Add the stock and honey, and cook for 3 to 4 minutes. Add the lemon juice, soy sauce, and chile sauce. Pour the glaze over the pork chops, and serve warm.

Heat the oil in a large ovenproof sauté pan over high heat until very hot. Add the endives and cook just until they start to brown, 2 to 3 minutes. Add the garlic, sherry, vinegar, stock, mustard, and butter, and bring the mixture to a boil. Cover the pan with a lid or foil, set it in the oven, and braise the endives for 10 to 15 minutes, until tender. Season to taste with salt and pepper.

To serve, place the endives on a serving platter and top with the braising liquid.

Cook One:

Make the stuffing.
Stuff the pork chops.
Sear the pork chops and finish cooking in the oven.
Finish the endives.
Plate the endives.

Cook Two:

Prep the pork chops.
Prep the endives.
Prep the ingredients for the ginger glaze.
Remove the pork chops from the pan and finish the glaze.
Plate and glaze the pork chops.

135

Menu 43:

Fettuccine with Bacon, Toasted Walnuts, and Blue Cheese

Balsamic-Dressed Greens

This is the perfect dinner for those times when we're sitting out on our deck in the early evening and our neighbors wander over for a glass of wine, which then transitions into a spur-of-the-moment dinner. For most of us, spur-of-the-moment means a menu hasn't been planned, requiring a foray into the pantry and the deep recesses of the refrigerator. That's why this pasta dish is so great, because everything needed to put it together—or fine substitutes—can be found in the barest of cupboards. When tossing the salad together, don't be tempted to reach for a premade dressing just to save time; it only takes a few moments to whisk together a better-than-bottled dressing. The dishes are so satisfying that you will want to plan a dinner party around them, just so you can serve them again. In a pinch, whatever wine you have on hand will be fine, but if you have a Bordeaux in your wine rack, open it for the perfect match.

Fettuccine with Bacon, Toasted Walnuts, and Blue Cheese

Serves 6

1 pound fettuccine
8 slices bacon, cubed
2 cloves garlic, chopped
$1/4$ cup extra virgin olive oil
2 tablespoons walnut oil
$1/2$ cup toasted walnuts (see page 188), chopped
4 ounces blue cheese, crumbled
Salt and freshly ground black pepper

Bring a large pot of salted water to a boil. Add the pasta and cook until al dente, about 8 minutes. Just before draining the pasta, ladle out $1/3$ cup of the cooking water and pour it in a large bowl; set aside. Drain the pasta well; set aside.

While the pasta is cooking, heat a large sauté pan over medium heat until very hot. Add the bacon and cook until crispy, about 4 minutes. Transfer the bacon to a paper towel to drain, reserving the drippings in the pan. Add the garlic to the pan and sauté for about 30 seconds. Add the olive oil and walnut oil, then remove the pan from the heat. Whisk the oil mixture into the reserved pasta water. Add the pasta and toss. Add the walnuts and blue cheese, and toss well. Season to taste with salt and pepper. Serve warm, garnished with the crispy bacon.

Balsamic-Dressed Greens

Serves 6

BALSAMIC DRESSING

2 tablespoons good-quality balsamic vinegar
    (aged 5 years)

1 clove garlic, chopped

3 shallots, roasted (see page 188) and chopped

1 heaping teaspoon Dijon mustard

1 teaspoon chopped fresh oregano

1 teaspoon chopped fresh basil

1 teaspoon chopped fresh sage

$^1/_3$ cup extra virgin olive oil

Salt and freshly ground black pepper

2 heads red-leaf lettuce or other seasonal greens, rinsed
    well, spun dry, and torn into bite-sized pieces

$^1/_4$ cup drained oil-packed sundried tomatoes, chopped

1 small red onion, julienned

$^1/_4$ cup chopped kalamata olives or other cured
    black olives

To prepare the dressing, whisk together the vinegar, garlic, shallots, mustard, oregano, basil, and sage in a small bowl. While whisking, slowly drizzle in the oil and whisk until smooth. Season to taste with salt and pepper; set aside.

To prepare the salad, in a large salad bowl, combine the lettuce, tomatoes, onion, and olives, and toss well. Add enough of the dressing to coat the greens, and toss well. Serve immediately.

Cook One:

Prep the greens and the other salad ingredients.

Cook the fettuccine.

Dress and plate the salad.

Cook Two:

Make the salad dressing.

Cook the bacon and make the pasta sauce.

Finish and plate the pasta.

Menu 44:

Lemongrass-Glazed New York Steak on Thai Noodle Salad

Since we are professional chefs, many people assume we eat lavish four-course meals every night. That may be true occasionally, but most nights we eat simply. However, simple for us doesn't mean flavorless and unimaginative. We always try to cook with seasonal ingredients and lots of vibrant flavors that come together easily, like in this colorful entrée salad. Several components make up this salad, many of which we like to prepare in advance—like making the dressing and glaze, prepping the vegetables, and cutting the garnishes. This way we're free to focus on grilling the steak before composing the salad with an artistic touch. With so much happening in the salad, we like to pour a Zinfandel, a robust varietal which can stand up to the assertive Asian flavors.

Lemongrass-Glazed New York Steak on Thai Noodle Salad

Serves 6

THAI NOODLE SALAD
6 large leaves romaine lettuce, rinsed well, spun dry, and julienned
1 (1-pound) package dried thin rice noodles
2 tomatoes, seeded (see page 188) and diced
1 large cucumber, diced
$^1/_2$ cup fresh basil leaves
$^1/_4$ cup fresh mint leaves
1 carrot, julienned
$^1/_4$ cup rice vinegar
1 tablespoon sugar
1 tablespoon peeled, grated fresh ginger
2 cloves garlic, chopped
1 tablespoon crushed red pepper flakes
$^3/_4$ cup vegetable oil, preferably canola
Soy sauce

STEAKS
1 cup sherry
2 cloves garlic, chopped
1 tablespoon minced fresh lemongrass
$^1/_3$ cup soy sauce
2 tablespoons honey
1 tablespoon Dijon mustard
$^1/_2$ teaspoon Asian chile sauce
3 (8-ounce) New York steaks
Salt and freshly ground black pepper

To prepare the salad, refrigerate the lettuce in a large bowl until you are ready to serve. In a large bowl, cover the noodles with warm water, and soak for 10 minutes to soften. Meanwhile, bring about 8 cups of salted water to a boil in a stockpot over high heat. Drain the noodles, add them to the boiling water, and cook just until tender, about 2 minutes. Drain the noodles, rinse

with cold water, then drain well. In a large bowl, combine the noodles, tomatoes, cucumber, basil, mint, and carrot, and toss well. Combine the vinegar, sugar, ginger, garlic, and pepper flakes in a bowl. While whisking, slowly add the oil, and whisk until smooth and emulsified. Season to taste with soy sauce. Pour the dressing over the noodles, toss well, and refrigerate until you are ready to serve.

To prepare the steaks, oil the grill and prepare a hot fire. If you are using a gas grill, preheat on high. If you are using a charcoal grill, let the coals burn until they are covered with gray ash. The fire is hot when you can hold your hand over the grill for no longer than 5 seconds.

Meanwhile, prepare the glaze. Combine the sherry, garlic, and lemongrass in a saucepan over medium heat and reduce until about $1/4$ cup of liquid remains, about 4 minutes. Transfer the mixture to a bowl, add the soy sauce, honey, mustard, and chile sauce, and whisk until smooth.

When the grill is hot, season the steaks with salt and pepper. Arrange the steaks on the grill and brush them with some of the glaze. Grill for about 4 minutes, then turn the steaks over and brush again with the glaze. Cook until the steaks reach an internal temperature of 135°F for medium doneness, about 4 minutes longer, depending on the thickness of the steaks. Let the steaks rest for about 3 minutes. Thinly slice the steaks.

To serve, divide the noodle salad among six large entrée plates. Distribute the lettuce over the salad, top with steak slices, drizzle with a bit of the remaining glaze, and serve immediately.

Cook One:

Soak the noodles for the salad.
Oil and light the grill.
Make the glaze for the steak.
Grill the steak.
Remove the steak from the grill and let it rest.

Cook Two:

Prep the vegetables for the salad.
Cook the noodles.
Finish preparing the noodle salad.
Plate the salad.
Slice the steak and place it on the salads.

139

Menu 45:

Port- and Soy-Glazed Beef Tenderloin

Mashed Butternut Squash
and Potatoes with Hazelnuts

Porcini Mushroom Compote

During the holiday season, we are so busy with the restaurant and cooking school that when we finally get to enjoy a dinner at home with our friends and family, we want to luxuriate in the time together. On the other hand, after doing so much cooking for other people, neither of us wants to spend all of Christmas day in the kitchen. A well-orchestrated menu like this one is vital for anyone putting together a festive meal. Both the side dishes can be done in advance and will hold well as you relax and sip champagne, and when it comes time to cook the tenderloin, at most you'll be away from the festivities for no more than 15 minutes. Porcini are our favorite mushrooms to use for this compote, but other seasonal varieties also will work nicely. This is the dinner that calls for a visit to the wine cellar for a special bottle you've been saving, such as a reserve Cabernet Sauvignon or an older Bordeaux.

Port- and Soy-Glazed Beef Tenderloin

Serves 6

1 tablespoon extra virgin olive oil
6 (6-ounce) beef tenderloins
Freshly ground black pepper
2 tablespoons unsalted butter
$^1/_4$ cup soy sauce
1 cup port

Preheat the oven to 400°F.

Heat the olive oil in a very large ovenproof sauté pan over high heat until smoking hot. Season the tenderloins heavily with pepper. Add the tenderloins to the pan and sear well, about 3 minutes per side. Set the pan in oven and roast the tenderloins until they reach an internal temperature of 130°F, about 6 minutes. Remove the pan from the oven and set it over high heat. Add the butter, soy sauce, and port, and cook until it thickens and coats the back of a spoon, about 3 minutes. Turn the tenderloins over to coat well with the sauce, then place on a serving platter. Drizzle with any remaining sauce. Serve hot.

Mashed Butternut Squash and Potatoes with Hazelnuts

Serves 6

1 small butternut squash (about $^1/_2$ pound), peeled and diced

1 $^1/_2$ pounds Yukon Gold potatoes, peeled and diced

4 whole cloves garlic

$^1/_2$ cup heavy whipping cream, warmed

2 tablespoons unsalted butter

Salt and freshly ground black pepper

$^1/_3$ cup ground toasted hazelnuts (see page 188)

Preheat the oven to 350°F. Combine the squash, potatoes, and garlic in a large saucepan, and add enough cold water to cover. Bring to a boil and cook over medium heat until the squash and potatoes are very tender, about 10 minutes. Drain well. Arrange in a single layer on a sheet pan, and bake for about 10 minutes to dry. Rice or mash the squash, potatoes, and garlic in a large bowl. Add the cream and butter, and mix well. Season to taste with salt and pepper. Fold in the toasted hazelnuts and mix well. Serve warm.

Porcini Mushroom Compote

Serves 6

2 tablespoons extra virgin olive oil

4 cups sliced porcini or other wild mushrooms

3 shallots, julienned

3 cloves garlic, chopped

$^1/_3$ cup brandy

$^1/_3$ cup dry sherry

1 teaspoon minced fresh rosemary

2 tablespoons unsalted butter

Salt and freshly ground black pepper

Heat the olive oil in a large sauté pan over high heat until very hot. Add the mushrooms and sauté until brown, about 4 minutes. Add the shallots, garlic, brandy, and sherry, cover the pan with a lid, and cook until the mushrooms are tender, about 5 minutes. Add the rosemary and butter, mix well, and season to taste with salt and pepper. Serve warm.

Cook One:

Peel the potatoes and squash and put them on to boil.

Finish the potatoes and squash and keep warm.

Sear, roast, and glaze the beef tenderloins.

Plate the beef tenderloin.

Cook Two:

Slice the mushrooms.

Finish the mushroom compote and keep warm.

Plate the potatoes and mushroom compote.

Open and pour the wine.

Curry-Rubbed Flank Steak with Plum Chutney

Menu 46:

Curry-Rubbed Flank Steak with Plum Chutney

Grilled Japanese Eggplant

Fragrant Noodles with Peanuts

When we set out to develop the recipes for this book, John insisted on plenty of grilled items. Two of his summertime favorites play an important role in tying this menu together and keeping him happily at the grill. We both think flank steak is one of the best meats to cook over a flame: it lends itself to cures and barbecue sauces, and, if cooked correctly, it is juicy and tender. We designed the eggplant recipe to be beautifully presented in a fan shapes, but if your knife does not cooperate, then just completely slice the eggplant through the stem end and worry about its presentation once it is on a plate. The noodle dish, with its crunchy peanuts and fragrant dressing, really should be served at room temperature instead of chilled, since the sauce tends to firm up too much when cold.

Curry-Rubbed Flank Steak with Plum Chutney

Serves 6

PLUM CHUTNEY
6 fresh plums, halved and diced
3 cloves garlic, minced
$1/2$ red onion, diced
1 $1/2$ teaspoons peeled, thinly sliced fresh ginger
$1/2$ cup mirin
$1/4$ cup sherry
2 tablespoons sweet soy sauce
1 tablespoon chopped fresh cilantro
Salt and freshly ground black pepper

STEAK
3 pounds flank steak
1 teaspoon kosher salt
1 tablespoon brown sugar
2 tablespoons curry powder

Cilantro sprigs, for garnish

To prepare the chutney, combine the plums, garlic, onion, ginger, mirin, sherry, and sweet soy sauce in a large saucepan over medium heat. Cook, stirring occasionally, until the plums are tender, about 10 minutes. Remove the pan from the heat, and stir in the cilantro. Season to taste with salt and pepper. Set aside until you are ready to serve.

To prepare the steak, oil the grill and prepare a hot fire. If you are using a gas grill, preheat on high. If you are using a charcoal grill, let the coals burn down until they are covered with gray ash. The fire is hot when you can hold your hand over the grill for no longer than 5 seconds.

Meanwhile, combine the salt, sugar, and curry powder in a small bowl, and mix well. Rub the flank steak well with the curry mixture. When the grill is hot, place the steak on the grill and grill for about 4 minutes per side for medium-rare doneness. Remove the steak from the grill and let it sit for about 4 minutes, then slice thinly against the grain at an angle.

To serve, place the steak on a serving platter, top with the chutney, and garnish with cilantro sprigs. Serve warm.

Cook One:

Make the chutney.
Make the dressing for the noodle salad.
Cook the noodles and finish the noodle salad.
Grill the eggplant and flank steak.
Plate and garnish the eggplant and the flank steak.

Cook Two:

Make the marinade and marinate the eggplant.
Oil and light the grill.
Rub the flank steak with the curry.
Plate and garnish the noodles.
Open and pour the wine.

Grilled Japanese Eggplant

Serves 6

6 Japanese eggplant
2 Anaheim chiles, roasted, peeled, and seeded (see page 187)
2 cloves garlic, chopped
2 tablespoons soy sauce
1 tablespoon honey
Juice and finely grated zest of 2 limes
2 tablespoons vegetable oil

Beginning about $1/2$ inch from the stem end, cut each eggplant into $1/2$-inch slices, making sure to keep the stem end intact. Place the eggplant on a sheet pan, then gently press on each one to fan the slices out.

To prepare the marinade, combine the chiles, garlic, soy sauce, honey, lime juice and zest, and vegetable oil in a blender, and blend until smooth. Place the eggplant in a baking dish, cover with the marinade, and marinate for about 1 hour.

While the eggplant marinates, oil the grill, and prepare a hot fire. If you are using a gas grill, preheat on high. If you are using a charcoal grill, let the coals burn down until they are covered with gray ash. The fire is hot when you can hold your hand over the grill for no longer than 5 seconds.

Remove the eggplant from the marinade and drain well. Place the eggplant on the grill, fanning the slices out, and grill until tender, about 4 minutes per side. Place on a serving platter. Serve warm.

Fragrant Noodles with Peanuts

Serves 6

1/4 cup cilantro leaves
1/4 cup basil leaves
1/2 cup roasted salted peanuts
2 tablespoon peeled, chopped fresh ginger
2 cloves garlic, chopped
1/4 cup red wine vinegar
Juice and finely grated zest of 1 lemon
1/4 cup soy sauce
1 cup vegetable oil, preferably canola
1 pound Chinese egg noodles
1/4 cup chopped roasted salted peanuts, for garnish
Cilantro or basil sprigs, for garnish

To make the dressing, combine the cilantro, basil, whole peanuts, ginger, garlic, vinegar, lemon juice and zest, soy sauce, and oil in a blender, and blend until smooth.

Bring a large pot of salted water to a boil. Add the noodles and cook until al dente, about 5 minutes. Drain well.

Transfer the noodles to a large bowl. Pour the dressing over the noodles and toss well.

To serve, transfer the noodles to a serving bowl, sprinkle with the chopped peanuts, and garnish with cilantro sprigs. Serve warm or at room temperature.

Menu 47:

Skirt Steak with Cappy's Barbecue Sauce

Herb Spaetzle

Spicy Cole Slaw

We wanted to include the definitive barbecue sauce in this book, but when it came time to develop the recipe, a friendly battle ensued. As self-anointed King of the Grill, John assumed that his concoction was the only choice, but Caprial had her own combination in mind. We seldom disagree on what goes into our recipes, so we decided to avoid havoc in the kitchen by including both recipes. This one, which begins with caramelized sugar and sweet onions, gives the steak a sweet-sour-smoky coating (find the other sauce recipe on page 129). The spaetzle, a tender dumpling, is made with a dough similar in consistency to pancake batter. Once the dumplings have been boiled and shocked in ice water, they can be kept refrigerated for two or three days before sautéing and serving. You can make the slaw as spicy or mild as your palate dictates by adding or omitting the jalapeño. As for the final element of this menu, we settled our differences by agreeing wholeheartedly on serving a cold microbrew.

Skirt Steak with Cappy's Barbecue Sauce

Serves 6

CAPPY'S BARBECUE SAUCE
1 cup sugar
1 large sweet onion, such as Walla Walla, finely diced
3 cloves garlic, chopped
$1/3$ cup plum vinegar or red wine vinegar
2 cups red wine
1 1/2 cups good-quality canned tomatoes
$1/3$ cup dark molasses
2 tablespoons Dijon mustard
$1/4$ cup Worcestershire sauce
2 tablespoons tomato paste
1 tablespoon ground cumin
1 tablespoon smoked paprika
1 tablespoon dried thyme
Juice and finely grated zest of 1 lemon
1 tablespoon cayenne sauce
Salt and freshly ground black pepper

3 pounds skirt steak
1 tablespoon extra virgin olive oil
Salt and freshly ground black pepper

To prepare the barbecue sauce, in a saucepan over high heat, cook the sugar, without stirring, until it starts to turn brown (all of the sugar does not need to caramelize before the onions are added). Add the onion and cook, again without stirring, until brown, 3 to 4 minutes. Add the garlic, vinegar, and wine, and reduce until the mixture is almost dry, about 5 minutes. Add the tomatoes, molasses, mustard, Worcestershire sauce, tomato paste, cumin, paprika, thyme, and the lemon juice and zest. Decrease the heat to medium-low and cook, stirring occasionally, for about 30 minutes. Transfer the sauce to a blender and purée. Add the cayenne sauce, blend to mix, and season to taste with salt and pepper. Refrigerate the sauce until you are ready to grill, reserving $1/2$ cup to serve on the side.

145

(continued)

(continued from page 145)

To prepare the steak, oil the grill and prepare a hot fire. If you are using a gas grill, preheat on high. If you are using a charcoal grill, let the coals burn down until they are covered with gray ash. The fire is hot when you can hold your hand over the grill for no longer than 5 seconds.

When the grill is hot, rub the steak with the oil and season well with salt and pepper. Place the steak on the grill and baste well with the barbecue sauce. Grill until the steak reaches an internal temperature of 130°F for medium-rare doneness, about 5 minutes per side, depending on the thickness of the steak. Remove from the grill and baste again. Let the steak rest for 3 to 5 minutes.

Slice the steak very thinly at an angle against the grain and place on a serving platter. Serve warm, with the reserved sauce on the side.

Herb Spaetzle

Serves 6

4 large eggs
$^1/_3$ cup milk
1 teaspoon chopped fresh thyme
1 teaspoon chopped fresh basil
1 teaspoon chopped fresh rosemary
1 $^1/_4$ cups all-purpose flour, plus more if needed
Salt and freshly ground black pepper
$^1/_4$ cup unsalted butter
2 teaspoons chopped garlic

To prepare the dough, whisk together the eggs and milk in a large bowl until smooth. Add the thyme, basil, and rosemary and mix well. Add the flour and mix well (the dough should be similar in consistency to pancake batter; add a couple of tablespoons more flour if the dough is too thin). Season well with salt and pepper.

To shape and cook the spaetzle, bring about 8 cups of salted water to a rolling boil in a stockpot over high heat. Fill a large bowl with ice water; set aside. Place the dough in a metal colander with medium-sized holes. While holding the colander over the boiling water and working quickly, use a rubber spatula to press all of the dough through the colander and into the boiling water. Cook for about 2 minutes, then transfer with a skimmer to the ice water to stop the cooking process. Drain well.

Heat the butter in a very large sauté pan over medium-high heat until bubbling and just beginning to turn brown. Add the spaetzle and garlic, and sauté just until the spaetzle starts to brown, about 4 minutes. Serve warm.

147

Spicy Cole Slaw

Serves 6

$^1/_2$ small head green cabbage, shredded
$^1/_2$ small head red cabbage, shredded
1 carrot, grated
1 red onion, julienned
3 cloves garlic, chopped
1 large egg yolk
2 jalapeños, minced
Juice and finely grated zest of 2 limes
2 tablespoons rice vinegar
$^2/_3$ cup extra virgin olive oil
$^1/_2$ teaspoon finely ground black pepper
Tabasco sauce
Salt

In a large bowl, toss together the cabbages, carrot, and onion; set aside.

To prepare the dressing, combine the garlic, egg yolk, jalapeños, lime juice and zest, and vinegar in a food processor and process until well blended. With the machine running, slowly add the olive oil and process until smooth and emulsified. Add the pepper, process to mix, and season to taste with Tabasco and salt.

Pour the dressing over the cabbage mixture and toss well. Refrigerate for at least 30 minutes or up to 24 hours before serving. Serve chilled.

Cook One:

Make the barbecue sauce.
Oil and light the grill.
Grill the steak.
Remove the steak from the grill and let rest.
Pour the reserved sauce into a sauce boat.
Slice and plate the steak.

Cook Two:

Make, boil, and shock the spaetzle.
Make the coleslaw and refrigerate.
Finish the spaetzle.
Plate the spaetzle and the coleslaw.
Open the cold beers.

<table>
<tr><td>

Menu 48:

Roasted Prime Rib with Pancetta

Carrot, Celeriac, and Sweet Potato
    Purée

Gingered Sugar Snap Peas

*Prime rib—a serious cut of beef—can be sea-
soned with just about anything, but if overcooked,
not even the best mixture of herbs and spices can
save it. If you are going to go to all the expense of
buying a well-marbled prime rib, we urge you to
buy an instant-read meat thermometer to ensure
that your time and effort don't go up in smoke. As
we direct in the recipe, it is necessary to remove
the rib from the oven as soon as it reaches 130°F
to insure that, when served, it will be about 135°F.
Tenting with foil and allowing it to rest for 5 to 10
minutes is the final step. As the meat sits, its tem-
perature raises 5 to 7 degrees, bringing it to a
perfect medium-rare. The side dishes in this
menu aren't as sensitive. We like to experiment
with other root vegetables in the purée, so each
time it comes out a bit different. The snap peas
give the menu a fresh hint of spice. A bold Caber-
net Sauvignon with a touch of oak will adorn the
meal with rich fruit and touches of vanilla.*

</td></tr>
</table>

Roasted Prime Rib with Pancetta

Serves 6

2 onions, coarsely chopped
3 carrots, coarsely chopped
4 stalks celery, coarsely chopped
6 cloves garlic, chopped
1 (5- to 6-pound) bone-in prime rib
Sea salt and freshly ground black pepper
2 tablespoons herb mustard, such as
    herbes de Provence
1 head garlic, roasted (see page 187)
1 tablespoon drained brined green peppercorns
1 tablespoon chopped fresh thyme
1 tablespoon chopped fresh marjoram
1 tablespoon chopped fresh basil
2 teaspoons chopped fresh rosemary
5 ($1/4$-inch-thick) slices pancetta

Preheat the oven to 425°F.

Combine the onions, carrots, celery, and garlic in a
large roasting pan. Season the prime rib well with sea
salt and pepper, then set it on top of the vegetables.
Combine the mustard, roasted garlic, and green peppercorns in a small bowl, mash together with a fork,
and then spread the mixture over the prime rib. Combine the thyme, marjoram, basil, and rosemary in a
small bowl and rub well into the roasted garlic mixture.
Unroll the pancetta and lay the strips over the top of
the prime rib, securing the ends with toothpicks.

Roast the prime rib for about 15 minutes, then
decrease the oven temperature to 300°F and roast the
beef until it reaches an internal temperature of about
130°F for medium-rare doneness, about 2 hours.

Remove the prime rib from the oven and let it rest for
about 10 minutes. Slice and place the meat on a serving platter. Serve warm.

149

Carrot, Celeriac, and Sweet Potato Purée

Serves 6

3 large carrots, diced
1 celeriac (celery root), peeled and diced
1 large sweet potato, diced
4 shallots, halved
2 tablespoons extra virgin olive oil
$^1/_2$ cup heavy whipping cream
2 tablespoons unsalted butter
3 cloves garlic, chopped
Salt and freshly ground black pepper

Preheat the oven to 425°F.

Place a roasting pan in the oven and preheat for about 10 minutes. Combine the carrots, celeriac, sweet potato, and shallots in a large bowl and toss well with the olive oil. Transfer the vegetables to the hot pan, shake the pan to spread them evenly, and roast, without stirring, for about 10 minutes. Toss and continue roasting until tender, about 10 minutes longer.

Transfer the vegetables to a large bowl and mash well, or place in a ricer and rice into a large bowl. Add the cream, butter, and garlic, and mix well. Season to taste with salt and pepper. Transfer to a serving bowl. Serve warm.

Gingered Sugar Snap Peas

Serves 6

1 tablespoon unsalted butter
1 $^1/_2$ pounds sugar snap peas, ends trimmed
2 cloves garlic, chopped
1 (1-inch) piece fresh ginger, peeled and julienned
1 tablespoon minced candied ginger
$^1/_3$ cup toasted slivered almonds (see page 188)
Salt and freshly ground black pepper

Heat the butter in a large sauté pan until melted and bubbling. Add the peas and sauté for about 3 minutes. Add the garlic and fresh ginger, and sauté for about 1 minute. Add the candied ginger and almonds, and sauté just until the peas are crisp-tender, about 1 minute. Season to taste with salt and black pepper. Transfer to a serving bowl. Serve warm.

Cook One:

Roast the garlic.

Place the prime rib in the roasting pan and season.

Finish seasoning the beef with the herbs and pancetta, and place in the oven.

Prep the snap peas.

When the vegetables are done, purée and keep them warm.

Cook the snap peas.

Plate the purée and the snap peas.

Open and serve the wine.

Cook Two:

Chop the vegetables for the prime rib.

Make the peppercorn mixture and season the beef with it.

Dice the vegetables for the purée.

Preheat a roasting pan and roast the vegetables.

When the beef reaches the correct internal temperature, remove from the oven and let rest.

Slice and plate the beef.

Menu 49:

Barbecued Chile-Rubbed Brisket with Honey-Bourbon Sauce

Grilled Red Potatoes with Mustard Vinaigrette

John's Sweet Pepper–Braised Corn

Everyone will agree that slow-cooked beef brisket is classic barbecue fare, but beyond that you'll find few concurring opinions. From sauce to condiments and even the type of fuel used for the fire, barbecue lovers will passionately defend their favorite style. That said, our barbecued brisket is coated with a smoky, chocolately rub that has a bit of kick, carefully tended over the coals, and then sliced and drizzled with a potent glaze. Further fights can erupt over the best potato salad, but we avoid any trappings of a traditional potato salad and take our spuds in a different direction. Boiled, tossed in a vinaigrette, and grilled to crispy perfection, the potatoes forever leave salad status behind. With all of the action on the barbecue, braising the corn in the oven gives the person tending the grill a break. A big, exuberant Zinfandel makes an agreeable match—and nobody will argue with that.

Barbecued Chile-Rubbed Brisket with Honey-Bourbon Sauce

Serves 6

CHILE RUB
$^1/_2$ cup firmly packed dark brown sugar
1 dried chipotle chile, pulverized
1 tablespoon ancho chile powder
1 tablespoon ground cumin
1 $^1/_2$ teaspoons onion powder
1 $^1/_2$ teaspoons garlic powder
1 teaspoon ground mace

1 (4- to 5-pound) beef brisket, trimmed
Salt and freshly ground black pepper

HONEY-BOURBON SAUCE
Juice of 2 lemons
$^1/_2$ cup good-quality bourbon
$^1/_4$ cup honey
1 tablespoon chopped fresh thyme
1 tablespoon Worcestershire sauce
1 teaspoon dry mustard
2 cloves garlic, chopped
Salt and freshly ground black pepper

To prepare the rub, combine the brown sugar, chipotle, chile powder, cumin, onion powder, garlic powder, and mace in a food processor and process until well blended. Place the brisket in a large nonreactive baking dish. Rub the brisket well with all of the chile rub. Cover with plastic wrap and refrigerate for at least 6 hours, and up to 24 hours.

To cook the brisket, oil the grill and prepare the coals by piling briquettes on one side of the barbecue and lighting them. Let them burn until they are gray in color, about 30 minutes. Season the brisket with salt and pepper, and place it skin side up on the opposite side of the grill from the coals. Set an oven thermometer in the barbecue, cover with the lid, and let the brisket roast until it reaches an internal temperature of 140°F,

151

(continued)

(continued from page 151)

about 4 hours. Try to keep the temperature of the barbecue at about 300°F. Add more briquettes if the fire starts to go out. If the temperature gets too high, partially close the air vent to lower the heat, but do not shut the vent completely or the fire will go out.

Just before the brisket is finished, make the sauce. Whisk together the lemon juice, bourbon, honey, thyme, Worcestershire sauce, mustard, and garlic in a bowl. Season to taste with salt and pepper. Set aside.

When the brisket is done, remove it from the barbecue, and let it rest for 5 to 10 minutes. Slice thinly against the grain. To serve, place the slices on a serving platter and drizzle with the sauce. Serve warm.

Grilled Red Potatoes with Mustard Vinaigrette

Serves 6

2 1/2 pounds small red potatoes, scrubbed
1/4 cup extra virgin olive oil
2 cloves garlic, chopped
2 tablespoons sherry vinegar
2 tablespoons dark molasses
1 tablespoon whole-grain mustard
2 teaspoons Dijon mustard
Salt and freshly ground black pepper

In a large stockpot combine the potatoes with enough cold water to cover, and bring to a boil over high heat. Decrease the heat to medium and simmer the potatoes until they are fork-tender, about 10 minutes. Drain the potatoes well, cut in half, and transfer to a large bowl.

In a small bowl, whisk together oil, garlic, vinegar, molasses, and mustards until smooth. Season to taste with salt and pepper. Pour the vinaigrette over the potatoes and let sit for at least 30 minutes, or up to 24 hours.

Prepare a hot fire in the grill. If you are using a gas grill, preheat on high. If you are using a charcoal grill, let the coals burn until they are covered with gray ash. The fire is hot when you can hold your hand over the grill for no longer than 5 seconds.

When the grill is hot, drain the potatoes well, reserving the vinaigrette in a large bowl. Oil a fine-mesh grate and place it over the hot coals. Transfer the potatoes to the grate and grill, turning occasionally, until well-browned, about 5 minutes. Transfer the potatoes to the reserved vinaigrette, and toss well. Place in a serving bowl and serve warm.

Cook One:

Cooks' Note: The brisket must cure for at least 6 hours, but no more than 24 hours, before cooking.

Oil and light the grill.

Place the brisket on the grill.

Prep the corn.

When the brisket reaches the correct internal temperature, remove from the grill and keep warm.

Grill the potatoes.

Plate the potatoes and corn.

Cook Two:

Cook the potatoes.

Make the vinaigrette, pour it over the potatoes, and refrigerate.

Make the bourbon sauce.

Cook the corn.

Slice, plate, and sauce the brisket.

Open and serve the wine.

John's Sweet Pepper–Braised Corn

Serves 6

3 slices bacon, diced
1 small red onion, diced
2 cloves garlic, chopped
2 red bell peppers, diced
4 ears white corn, shucked and cut into thirds
1 teaspoon mild chile powder
1 teaspoon ground cumin
$^1/_2$ cup vegetable stock (page 186) or chicken stock (page 184)
Salt and freshly ground black pepper

Preheat the oven to 375°F.

Heat a large straight-sided, ovenproof sauté pan over medium heat until hot. Add the bacon and cook until very crispy, about 4 minutes. Transfer the bacon to a paper towel to drain, reserving the drippings in the pan. Add the onion and garlic to the pan, and sauté for about 2 minutes. Add the bell peppers and sauté for about 2 minutes. Add the corn, chile powder, cumin, and stock, and bring to a boil. Cover the pan with a lid, set it in the oven, and braise the corn until tender, 12 to 15 minutes. Season to taste with salt and lots of pepper.

To serve, spoon the corn onto a serving platter, pour the braising liquid over the top, and garnish with the crispy bacon. Serve warm.

153

Menu 50:

Osso Buco Braised with Mint and Tomatoes

Green Beans Glazed with Balsamic Vinegar

Looking back at all the recipes we've created over the years, we realized that braised shanks—either osso buco or lamb shanks—comprise such a large section that we have enough to fill an entire book on the subject. We just can't imagine our cooking repertoire without this indispensable method that turns inexpensive cuts of lamb or veal into sheer comfort food. We've extolled its virtues in every one of our books, so we'll keep it simple: This is a dish we really love to eat and share with our friends. A French Corbières, a somewhat esoteric wine with black pepper nuances, is the wine we paired with this latest take on a family favorite.

Osso Buco Braised with Mint and Tomatoes

Serves 4

4 (10- to 12-ounce) veal shanks
Salt and freshly ground black pepper
1 cup all-purpose flour
2 tablespoons extra virgin olive oil
2 onions, julienned
2 cloves garlic, chopped
1 cup red wine
1 tablespoon chopped fresh mint
2 tomatoes, seeded (see page 188) and chopped
8 small red potatoes, halved
3 cups chicken stock (page 184)
$1/2$ cup sour cream, for garnish
1 tablespoon ground cumin, for garnish

Preheat the oven to 350°F.

Season the shanks with salt and pepper and dredge them in the flour, shaking off the excess. Heat the oil in a roasting pan set over high heat until smoking hot. Add the shanks and brown well, about 3 minutes per side. Transfer to a plate and set aside. Add the onions to the pan, decrease the heat to medium, and cook, stirring once or twice, until golden brown, about 15 minutes. Add the garlic and cook for 1 minute, then add the shanks and red wine and reduce over high heat until about $1/2$ cup of wine remains, about 4 minutes. Add the mint, tomatoes, potatoes, and chicken stock, and season with salt and pepper. Cover the pan with a lid or foil, set it in the oven, and cook the shanks until tender, about 1 hour.

To serve, combine the sour cream and cumin in a small bowl and mix well. Serve the veal shanks and vegetables hot, garnished with a dollop of the sour cream.

Green Beans Glazed with Balsamic Vinegar

Serves 6

1 1/2 pounds fresh green beans, trimmed
2 teaspoons unsalted butter
1 clove garlic, minced
2 tablespoons good-quality (aged at least 5 years)
    balsamic vinegar
2 dashes of soy sauce

In a large pan over high heat, bring about 5 cups of salted water to a rolling boil. Add the beans and cook until they are crisp-tender, about 4 minutes. Drain the beans and then immediately shock them in ice water to stop the cooking process. Drain well.

Heat the butter in a sauté pan over medium heat until melted and bubbling. Add the garlic and beans and toss to coat with the butter. Add the vinegar and soy sauce, toss well, and cook until the beans are hot, 3 to 4 minutes. Transfer to a serving platter. Serve hot.

Cook One:

Season and sear the veal shanks.

Finish preparing the braising liquid, and place the shanks in the oven.

Make the green beans.

Plate the green beans.

Cook Two:

Prep the vegetables for the braising liquid.

While the veal shanks are braising, pour two glasses of red wine to share with Cook One.

Make the sour cream, and plate and garnish the veal shanks.

Desserts

Blackberry Pie with Cornmeal Streusel

Serves 10

CRUST

1 1/3 cups all-purpose flour

1/2 teaspoon salt

1/4 cup cold unsalted butter, diced

1/4 cup vegetable shortening

6 tablespoons ice water

FILLING

5 cups fresh blackberries

1 cup sugar

1 teaspoon pure vanilla extract

Finely grated zest of 1 lemon

2 tablespoons cornstarch

1 teaspoon ground cinnamon

1/2 teaspoon ground ginger

CORNMEAL STREUSEL

1/4 cup unsalted butter

1/3 cup flour

1/4 cup finely ground cornmeal

1/4 cup sugar

Pinch of salt

1 quart vanilla ice cream, as accompaniment

To prepare the crust, combine the flour, salt, butter, and shortening in a bowl. Using your fingertips, blend until the mixture resembles a coarse meal. Add the water and mix with a fork just until the dough is moistened and comes together. Turn the dough out onto a well-floured board, form it into a disk with your hands, and wrap in plastic wrap. Refrigerate for 30 minutes.

Preheat the oven to 425°F.

On a well-floured board, roll out the dough to a 10-inch circle. Fit the dough into a 9-inch pie plate, fold the edges under, and flute. In a large bowl, combine the berries, sugar, vanilla extract, lemon zest, cornstarch, cinnamon, and ginger. Mix well. Pour the filling into the crust; set aside.

To prepare the streusel, combine the butter, flour, cornmeal, sugar, and salt in a small bowl. Using your fingertips, mix just until crumbly. Sprinkle the streusel over the berries.

Bake the pie for 15 minutes, then decrease the oven temperature to 350°F and bake for about 40 minutes longer, until golden brown and bubbly.

Let the pie cool for about 20 minutes before serving. Serve warm with vanilla ice cream.

Raspberry Cream Tart

Serves 12

PÂTE BRISÉE CRUST

1 ¹/₂ cups all-purpose flour

¹/₂ teaspoon salt

¹/₂ teaspoon sugar

3 tablespoons vegetable shortening

¹/₂ cup cold unsalted butter, diced

¹/₄ cup ice water

FILLING

2 cups mascarpone (page 182)

¹/₂ cup sugar

¹/₂ teaspoon pure vanilla extract

¹/₂ teaspoon lemon oil

Juice of ¹/₂ lemon

Finely grated zest of 1 lemon

1 cup softly whipped cream

2 pints fresh raspberries, plus extra for garnish, if desired

Confectioners' sugar, for dusting

Mint sprigs, for garnish

Preheat the oven to 425°F.

To prepare the crust, combine the flour, salt, and sugar in the bowl of a mixer fitted with the paddle attachment and mix on low speed to combine. With the mixer on low speed, add the shortening and butter, and mix just until the mixture resembles a coarse meal. Add the ice water and mix just until the dough starts to come together. Turn the dough out onto a well-floured board and form it into a disk with your hands. Roll the dough out into a 12-inch circle and fit it into a 10-inch tart or flan pan with a removable bottom. Bake for 20 to 25 minutes, until golden brown. Let cool completely.

While the crust is cooling, stir the mascarpone in a large bowl to soften it. Add the sugar, vanilla extract, lemon oil, lemon juice and zest, and mix well. Gently fold in the whipped cream just until incorporated. Pour the filling into the cooled tart shell. Scatter the raspberries over the filling. Refrigerate for about 20 minutes to chill.

Serve cold, dusted with confectioners' sugar and garnished with mint sprigs and more fresh raspberries.

Baked Strawberry Tart

Serves 10

Quick Puff Pastry (page 182)
1 large egg, beaten
2 pints strawberries, hulled and halved
³/₄ cup superfine sugar
1 teaspoon pure vanilla extract
1 tablespoon cornstarch
¹/₄ cup Tuaca (citrus-flavored Italian liqueur)
1 tablespoon minced candied ginger

TOPPING
1 ¹/₂ cups crème fraîche (page 181)
¹/₃ cup superfine sugar

Mint sprigs, for garnish

Preheat the oven to 375°F. Line a sheet pan with parchment paper.

To prepare the tart, on a well-floured board, roll out the puff pastry into a 12-inch square. Starting 1 inch diagonally from one corner, use a sharp knife to make a 10-inch-long cut parallel to the edge of the pastry, stopping within 1 inch from the end. Next, beginning in the same corner as the original cut, make another 10-inch-long cut along the edge perpendicular to the original cut. Repeat the procedure in the opposite corner. You should end up with a partially cut square 1 inch smaller than the 12-inch square of pastry. Brush the 1-inch-wide strip of pastry with some of the beaten egg, then carefully lift it at one corner and fold over to the opposite inner corner. Press to seal. Repeat with the opposite corner. Place the tart shell on the prepared sheet pan and brush it with the remaining beaten egg. Refrigerate the tart shell until you are ready to bake.

To assemble the tart, combine the strawberries, sugar, vanilla extract, cornstarch, and Tuaca in a large bowl, and mix well. Starting at one edge of the tart shell and working your way down, arrange the strawberry halves, cut side down, in straight rows. Drizzle the berries with any sugar mixture that remains in the bowl. Bake the tart for 40 to 50 minutes, until the strawberries are tender and bubbling. Let cool on the pan for 10 to 15 minutes.

While the tart is cooling, make the topping. Combine the crème fraîche and sugar in a small bowl, and mix well.

To serve, slice the tart into squares. Serve warm, drizzled with the sweetened crème fraîche and garnished with mint sprigs.

Pear Tart with Chocolate Cookie Crust

Serves 12

4 semi-ripe pears, peeled, cored, and halved
5 cups dry white wine
Finely grated zest of 1 orange
1 1/2 cups sugar
1 cup heavy whipping cream
3 large eggs
1 teaspoon pure vanilla extract
Pinch of nutmeg
Pinch of salt
Confectioners' sugar, for dusting

CHOCOLATE COOKIE CRUST

2 cups chocolate cookie crumbs (such as Famous Chocolate Wafers)
2 tablespoons sugar
1 teaspoon ground cinnamon
6 tablespoons unsalted butter, melted

Preheat the oven to 350°F. Grease a 10-inch flan or tart pan with a removable bottom.

To poach the pears, combine the pears, wine, orange zest, and $3/4$ cup of the sugar in a large saucepan over high heat, and bring to a boil. Decrease the heat and simmer until the pears are fork tender, about 15 minutes. Remove the pan from the heat, and let the pears cool in the liquid.

While the pears are cooling, prepare the crust. Combine the cookie crumbs with the sugar and cinnamon in a large bowl. Add the butter and mix just until the crust holds together. Press the crust into the prepared pan.

Using a slotted spoon, remove the pears from the liquid and drain well (reserve the poaching liquid in the pan). Slice the pears into $1/4$-inch-thick slices. Arrange the slices in concentric circles on the prepared crust; set aside. In a large bowl, whisk together the cream, eggs, remaining $3/4$ cup sugar, and the vanilla extract, nutmeg, and salt. Pour the mixture over the pears, and bake for about 40 minutes, until the custard is just set. Let cool while you prepare the sauce.

While the tart is cooling, set the pan of poaching liquid over medium heat and reduce until about $1 1/2$ cups of liquid remain, about 15 minutes. Strain through a fine-mesh sieve.

To serve, slice the tart, dust with confectioners' sugar, and drizzle with the warm sauce.

161

Jam Tart

Serves 10

CRUST

3 cups all-purpose flour

1¼ cup toasted finely ground almonds (see page 188)

⅔ cup superfine sugar

2 teaspoons baking powder

2 large eggs

2 teaspoons finely grated lemon zest

½ teaspoon salt

⅔ cup unsalted butter, melted

1 ½ cups high-quality fruit jam

1 quart vanilla ice cream, as accompaniment

Mint sprigs, for garnish

To prepare the crust, combine the flour, almonds, sugar, and baking powder in a food processor, and pulse to mix. Add the egg and pulse again until the mixture resembles coarse crumbs. Add the lemon zest, salt, and butter, and pulse again just until a soft dough forms. Form the dough into a disk, wrap in plastic wrap, and refrigerate until the dough is chilled and easier to handle, about 30 minutes.

Preheat the oven to 350°F. Grease a 10-inch tart or flan pan with a removable bottom.

To assemble the tart, press the dough into the prepared pan and trim the edges, saving the excess dough. Spread the jam over the bottom of the crust. Roll out the remaining dough and cut it into eight ½-inch-wide strips. Lay four strips diagonally across the top of the tart, then lay the remaining four strips across the tart to form a lattice. Trim the edges if needed.

Bake the tart for about 30 minutes, until the crust is golden brown and the jam is bubbling slightly. Let cool for about 10 minutes before serving. Serve warm with vanilla ice cream and fresh mint.

Lemon Crème Brûlée Tart

Serves 12

NUT CRUST

1 ¹/₂ cups all-purpose flour

¹/₄ cup toasted ground almonds (see page 188)

¹/₄ cup toasted ground cashews (see page 188)

¹/₄ cup toasted ground hazelnuts (see page 188)

¹/₂ cup sugar

1 teaspoon pure vanilla extract

1 teaspoon ground cinnamon

¹/₂ teaspoon salt

1 cup unsalted butter, at room temperature

LEMON CRÈME BRÛLÉE FILLING

3 cups heavy whipping cream

Finely grated zest of 2 lemons

¹/₂ vanilla bean, split in half lengthwise

6 large egg yolks

¹/₃ cup sugar

¹/₃ cup superfine sugar

Softly whipped cream, as accompaniment

Fresh berries, as accompaniment

To prepare the crust, combine the flour, almonds, cashews, hazelnuts, sugar, vanilla extract, cinnamon, and salt in a food processor and process to mix. With the motor running, slowly add the butter, a bit at a time, and process until the dough forms on top of the blades. Remove the dough from the food processor, roll it into a ball, wrap it in plastic wrap, and refrigerate it until it is chilled and easier to handle, about 30 minutes.

While the dough is chilling, preheat the oven to 375°F (you will get the best results in a convection oven). Grease a 10-inch springform pan.

Press the dough into the bottom and about halfway up the sides of the prepared pan. Bake until set, about 10 minutes. Let cool completely.

While the crust is cooling, prepare the filling. Combine the cream, lemon zest, and vanilla bean in a heavy saucepan over medium heat and bring just to a boil. Remove the pan from the heat, cover, and let the mixture steep for about 30 minutes.

Bring the mixture back up to a boil, then remove the pan from the heat. Meanwhile, combine the egg yolks and sugar in a bowl, and whisk until smooth. While whisking, slowly add about 1 cup of the hot cream into the egg mixture to temper it, or bring it up to the same temperature. Whisk in the remaining cream. Scrape the seeds from the inside of the vanilla bean into the custard (discard the bean), mix gently, then skim any foam from the surface.

Reduce the oven temperature to 325°F. Pour the filling into the cooled shell, and bake for about 45 minutes, until the custard is set. Let cool for about 20 minutes, then refrigerate until chilled, 2 hours.

To serve, sprinkle the tart with the superfine sugar. Using a propane torch (but not the broiler, because it will make the filling too soft), caramelize the sugar. Slice and serve with softly whipped cream and fresh berries.

Coconut Cream Cheesecake with Almond Crust and Chocolate Sauce

Serves 12

ALMOND CRUST

3 cups ground toasted almonds (see page 188)

$^1/_4$ cup sugar

$^1/_2$ teaspoon almond extract

6 tablespoons unsalted butter, melted

FILLING

2 pounds cream cheese, at room temperature

1 $^1/_2$ cups sugar

1 cup coconut milk

4 large eggs, separated

$^1/_2$ teaspoon pure vanilla extract

1 $^3/_4$ cups shredded sweetened coconut, toasted (see page 187)

Pinch of salt

CHOCOLATE SAUCE

$^1/_2$ cup unsalted butter

1 cup sugar

1 cup heavy whipping cream

$^1/_3$ cup unsweetened cocoa powder

Pinch of salt

1 tablespoon pure vanilla extract

2 cups softly whipped cream, as accompaniment

Preheat the oven to 300°F. Grease a 10-inch springform pan.

To prepare the crust, combine the almonds, sugar, and almond extract in a bowl, and mix well. Add the butter and mix to moisten. Press the crust into the bottom and about halfway up the sides of the prepared pan. Refrigerate the crust while you prepare the filling.

To prepare the filling, combine the cream cheese, sugar, and coconut milk in a food processor and process until the mixture is very smooth, and there are no lumps of cream cheese, scraping down the sides of the bowl often. Add the egg yolks and vanilla extract, and process until very smooth; transfer to a bowl. In the clean bowl of a mixer fitted with the whip attachment, whip the egg whites on high speed until they hold soft peaks. Fold 1 $^1/_2$ cups of the coconut into the cream cheese mixture, reserving $^1/_4$ cup for garnish. Gently fold in the egg whites. Pour the filling into the prepared crust and bake for about 1 hour, until the cheesecake is just set. Let the cheesecake cool for about 30 minutes, then refrigerate for about 4 hours until chilled.

Meanwhile, to prepare the chocolate sauce, combine the butter, sugar, cream, and cocoa powder in a heavy saucepan over medium heat and bring just to a boil, stirring often. Decrease the heat to low and simmer, stirring often, until the mixture is thick and coats the back of a spoon, about 7 minutes. Remove the pan from the heat and stir in the salt and vanilla extract. Let cool for about 5 minutes before using. (The sauce will keep, refrigerated, for up to 1 week. Gently warm the chilled sauce in a heavy saucepan over low heat, or in a microwave on low power.)

Serve the cheesecake chilled, topped with warm chocolate sauce and softly whipped cream, and garnished with the reserved $^1/_4$ cup toasted coconut.

Individual Chocolate-Orange Cakes

Serves 12

14 ounces bittersweet chocolate, coarsely chopped

1 1/4 cups unsalted butter, at room temperature

1 cup sugar

1/3 cup dark rum

1/2 teaspoon pure vanilla extract

6 large eggs

Finely grated zest of 1 orange

1/2 teaspoon orange oil

2/3 cup flour

Pinch of salt

Confectioners' sugar, for dusting

1 1/2 cups chocolate sauce (page 164),
    as accompaniment

1 1/2 cups softly whipped cream,
    as accompaniment

Preheat the oven to 350°F. Grease twelve 8-ounce ramekins.

Place the chocolate and butter in a metal bowl set over a pan of simmering water. Once the chocolate has melted about halfway, remove the pan from the heat (leave the bowl on the pan), and let the chocolate finish melting.

Combine the sugar, rum, and vanilla extract in the bowl of a mixer fitted with the whip attachment and beat, scraping down the sides of the bowl often, until very light and fluffy, about 5 minutes. With the mixer on low speed, add the eggs, one at a time, scraping down the sides of the bowl and mixing well after each addition. Add the orange zest, orange oil, flour, and salt, and mix on low speed just until the batter is combined. Add the chocolate mixture and mix just until the batter is well blended.

Divide the batter among the prepared ramekins. Place the ramekins in a shallow roasting pan, and fill the pan with enough hot water to reach about halfway up the sides of the ramekins. Carefully set the pan in the oven and bake for about 30 minutes, until a skewer inserted in the cakes comes out covered in moist crumbs. Let cool in the ramekins for about 10 minutes, then remove from the ramekins.

To serve, set each cake on plate, dust with confectioners' sugar, drizzle with chocolate sauce, and top with whipped cream. Serve warm or at room temperature.

Apple-Yogurt Cakes

Makes 12

1 cup unsalted butter, at room temperature

2 cups sugar

4 large eggs

2 teaspoons pure vanilla extract

1 teaspoon orange oil (optional)

Finely grated zest of 1 orange

1 teaspoon ground cinnamon

1 tablespoon minced candied ginger

1 teaspoon baking soda

1 teaspoon baking powder

1 cup plain whole-milk yogurt

2 tart baking apples, such as Granny Smith or
     Gravenstein, peeled, cored, and diced

2 1/2 cups all-purpose flour

1 teaspoon salt

1/2 cup confectioners' sugar, for dusting

Preheat the oven to 350°F. Grease 12 large muffin cups.

Combine the butter and sugar in the bowl of a mixer fitted with the paddle attachment and beat on high speed, scraping down the sides of the bowl occasionally, until very light and fluffy. With the mixer on low speed, add the eggs, one at a time, scraping down the sides of the bowl and mixing well after each addition. Add the vanilla extract, orange oil, orange zest, cinnamon, and candied ginger, and mix well. Add the baking soda and baking powder, and mix well. Add the yogurt and mix well, scraping down the sides of the bowl. Add the apples, mix well, and then add the flour and salt, and mix until smooth. Pour the batter into the prepared muffin cups.

Bake for about 40 minutes, until a skewer inserted in the cakes comes out covered in moist crumbs. Let cool for about 5 minutes, and then remove the cakes from the pan and let cool completely.

To serve, place each cake on a plate and dust with confectioners' sugar.

Spice Sable Cookies

Makes about 24 cookies

1 1/4 cups sugar
1/2 cup unsalted butter, at room temperature
1 large egg yolk
Finely grated zest of 1 orange
1/2 teaspoon orange oil
1/2 teaspoon ground cinnamon
1/4 teaspoon ground ginger
1/4 teaspoon ground nutmeg
1/4 teaspoon ground allspice
1 1/4 cups all-purpose flour
Pinch of salt

Combine 1/4 cup of the sugar and the butter in the bowl of a mixer fitted with the paddle attachment, and beat on high speed, scraping down the sides of the bowl often, until light and fluffy, about 4 minutes. Add the egg yolk, orange zest, orange oil, cinnamon, ginger, nutmeg, and allspice. Mix well. Add the flour and salt, start the mixer very slowly (so you don't end up wearing the flour), and mix on low speed until smooth. Gather the dough into a ball, wrap in plastic wrap, and refrigerate until well chilled, about 1 hour.

Preheat the oven to 350°F. Grease a sheet pan well.

Rinse a 5 by 5-inch square of cheesecloth in water and wring out so that it is just damp. Place the cheesecloth around the bottom of a flat-bottom glass and secure it with a rubber band. Place the remaining 1 cup sugar on a plate. Shape the dough into 1/2-inch balls. Place one ball of dough on the prepared pan. Dip the bottom of the glass in the sugar and press it onto the dough to flatten it into a 3-inch cookie. Place the next ball of dough on the pan and repeat the process, making sure the cookies are spaced about 1/2 inch apart. Continue until the pan is full.

Bake the cookies for about 12 minutes, until golden brown. Lift the cookies with a spatula to loosen, then cool completely on the pan.

Mocha-Chocolate Chunk Cookies

Makes about 24 cookies

1 cup unsalted butter, at room temperature
1 teaspoon pure vanilla extract
1 cup white sugar
1/2 cup firmly packed dark brown sugar
2 tablespoons instant espresso powder
2 large eggs
1 3/4 cups all-purpose flour
3/4 cup cocoa powder
1/2 teaspoon salt
1/2 cup toasted hazelnuts (see page 188), chopped
8 ounces bittersweet chocolate, chopped

Preheat the oven to 350°F. Grease a sheet pan well.

Combine the butter, vanilla extract, white sugar, brown sugar, and instant espresso powder in the bowl of a mixer fitted with the paddle attachment. Beat on high speed, scraping down the sides of the bowl often, until light and fluffy, about 4 minutes. With the mixer on low speed, add the eggs and beat well. Add the flour, cocoa powder, and salt, and mix on low speed until all the ingredients are well incorporated. Add the hazelnuts and chocolate, and mix just until smooth.

Place heaping tablespoonfuls of the dough about 1 inch apart on the prepared pan. Bake for about 10 minutes, just until set. (If you aren't sure if the cookies are done, it's better to pull them out of the oven sooner rather then later.) Let the cookies cool on the pan for a few minutes, then transfer to a rack or paper towels and let cool completely. Store in an airtight container for up to 3 days.

Note: These brownielike cookies do not require a leavener.

White Chocolate Semifreddo

Serves 6

5 large eggs, separated
1/2 cup sugar
1 teaspoon pure vanilla extract
6 ounces white chocolate, melted
2 cups heavy whipping cream
1 tablespoon minced candied ginger
Fresh berries, as accompaniment
Mint sprigs, for garnish

Combine the egg yolks, sugar, and vanilla extract in the bowl of a mixer fitted with the whip attachment, and whip on high speed until very light and fluffy, 3 to 5 minutes. Gently fold in the melted chocolate; set aside.

In a large bowl, whisk the cream just until it starts to thicken, then gently fold in the egg yolk mixture and the candied ginger.

In a clean bowl of a mixer fitted with the whip attachment, whip the egg whites on high speed until they just hold soft peaks. Gently fold the whites into the egg yolk mixture. Transfer the mixture to a covered container and freeze for at least 2 hours.

Scoop and serve with fresh berries and mint sprigs.

Oven-Braised Peaches with Raspberry Sorbet

Serves 6

RASPBERRY SORBET
4 cups raspberry purée
1 ³/₄ cups sugar
Juice of ¹/₂ lemon
¹/₄ cup heavy whipping cream

PEACHES
2 tablespoons unsalted butter
¹/₂ teaspoon minced or grated peeled, fresh ginger
1 star anise
³/₄ cup sugar
6 ripe peaches, peeled (see page 188) and halved
1 (750-ml) bottle good-quality Riesling wine

To prepare the sorbet, combine the raspberry purée and sugar in a saucepan over high heat. Bring to a boil and cook until the sugar is dissolved, about 3 minutes. Add the lemon juice and cream, and cook for about 2 minutes longer. Remove the pan from the heat, and refrigerate until the mixture cools to at least 40°F, about 2 hours. To freeze the sorbet, follow the manufacturer's directions for your ice-cream maker.

To prepare the peaches, preheat the oven to 350°F.

Heat the butter in a large ovenproof sauté pan over medium heat until melted and bubbling. Add the ginger and star anise, and sauté for about 30 seconds. Add the sugar and peaches, cover with the wine, and cook just until the wine comes to a boil. Cover the pan with a lid, set it in the oven, and braise the peaches for about 30 minutes, until tender. Using a slotted spoon, remove the peaches from the braising liquid, and place them on a plate; set aside.

Set the pan of braising liquid over high heat and reduce until about 1 cup remains, about 8 minutes.

To serve, place a scoop of raspberry sorbet on each plate. Arrange 2 peach halves on each side of the sorbet. Drizzle with the warm braising liquid, and serve immediately.

Note: The sorbet recipe makes 1 ¹/₂ quarts. Any leftover sorbet can be saved in the freezer for up to 6 months.

Chocolate Fondue

Serves 6

CHOCOLATE FONDUE

1 cup heavy whipping cream

1 teaspoon pure vanilla extract

$^1/_3$ cup hazelnut liqueur

2 tablespoons unsalted butter

5 ounces bittersweet chocolate, coarsely chopped

5 ounces hazelnut chocolate, coarsely chopped

1 pint fresh strawberries, hulled, as accompaniment

6 slices pound cake, cut into large dice, as accompaniment

2 bananas, peeled and cut into large dice, as accompaniment

Combine the cream, vanilla extract, liqueur, and butter in a heavy saucepan over medium heat and bring just to a boil. Place both chocolates in a food processor and process until finely chopped. With the motor running, slowly pour the hot cream mixture through the feed tube and process until smooth. Transfer the mixture to a fondue pot set over low heat, or keep warm until you are ready to serve.

Serve warm with skewered strawberries, pound cake, and bananas.

Dessert Bruschetta with Chocolate Ganache, Strawberries, and Hazelnuts

Serves 6

$^2/_3$ cup heavy whipping cream

6 ounces hazelnut chocolate or bittersweet chocolate, coarsely chopped

6 ($^1/_2$-inch-thick) slices rich, slightly sweet egg bread, such as brioche or challah

2 tablespoons unsalted butter, melted

1 pint fresh strawberries, hulled and sliced

$^1/_2$ cup shaved white chocolate (see page 187)

$^1/_3$ cup chopped toasted hazelnuts (see page 188)

Mint sprigs, for garnish

To prepare the ganache, in a heavy saucepan over medium heat, bring the cream just to a boil. Process the chocolate in a food processor until finely chopped. With the motor running, slowly pour the hot cream through the feed tube and process until smooth. Transfer the ganache to a bowl, and let cool until tepid.

While the ganache is cooling, oil the grill and prepare a hot fire. If you are using a gas grill, preheat on high. If you are using a charcoal grill, let the coals burn until they are covered with gray ash. The fire is very hot when you can hold your hand over the grill for no longer than 5 seconds.

To prepare the bruschetta, brush the bread slices on both sides with the melted butter. Place the bread on the grill and cook until toasted and golden brown, about 2 minutes per side.

To finish the dish, in the bowl of a mixer fitted with the whip attachment, whip the cooled ganache until light and fluffy. Generously spread each slice of bruschetta with whipped ganache. Arrange the strawberries over the ganache. Cut the bruschetta in half at an angle, then top with the shaved chocolate and sprinkle with the hazelnuts.

To serve, place the bruschetta on a serving platter or on individual plates, and garnish with mint sprigs.

Cherry-Almond Gratins

Serves 6

1/4 cup unsalted butter
6 cups fresh cherries, pitted
1 1/4 cups sugar
1 1/2 cups toasted ground almonds (see page 188)
8 large egg yolks
1/2 teaspoon almond extract
1/2 cup almond liqueur
Pinch of salt
1 quart vanilla ice cream, as accompaniment
Mint sprigs, for garnish

Butter six 8-ounce ramekins, using about 2 tablespoons of the butter.

Heat the remaining 2 tablespoons butter in a large sauté pan over medium-high heat until melted and bubbling. Add the cherries and 1/2 cup of the sugar, and cook until the cherries are tender, about 5 minutes. Remove the pan from the heat, then stir in the almonds. Divide the cherries among the prepared ramekins.

Preheat the broiler.

In a large metal bowl, whisk together the remaining 3/4 cup sugar and the egg yolks, almond extract, liqueur, and salt. Set the bowl over a pan of simmering water (make sure the bottom of the bowl does not touch the water), and cook, whisking constantly, until the mixture is very thick, like softly whipped cream, about 5 minutes. Distribute the egg yolk mixture over the cherries. Set the ramekins under the broiler and broil until golden brown, 3 to 4 minutes.

To serve, set each ramekin on a plate, top with a scoop of ice cream, and garnish with mint sprigs. Serve warm.

Caramel Pudding with Macerated Strawberries

Serves 6

STRAWBERRIES

3 cups sliced fresh strawberries

$1/4$ cup sugar

$1/2$ teaspoon pure vanilla extract

$1/4$ cup ground nutmeg

$1/3$ cup Tuaca (citrus-flavored Italian liqueur)

CARAMEL PUDDING

4 cups half-and-half

4 large egg yolks

$1/4$ cup cornstarch

2 teaspoons pure vanilla extract

Pinch of salt

1 cup sugar

1 cup water

$1/4$ cup cold unsalted butter, diced

1 $1/2$ cups softly whipped cream, as accompaniment

Mint sprigs, for garnish

To prepare the strawberries, combine the strawberries, sugar, vanilla extract, nutmeg, and Tuaca in a bowl, and mix well. Let stand at room temperature to allow the strawberries to marinate.

While the strawberries are marinating, prepare the pudding. Whisk together 2 cups of the half-and-half and the egg yolks, cornstarch, vanilla extract, and salt in a large bowl; set aside.

In a large sauté pan with sides or a heavy saucepan, moisten the sugar with the water, being very careful not to splash the water and sugar onto the sides of the pan. Cook the sugar mixture over high heat, without stirring, until you see any part of it turning brown, then swirl the pan to even out the color. Cook until golden brown, about 2 minutes longer. Carefully add the remaining 2 cups half-and-half to the hot sugar, taking care to pour it in slowly because it will bubble up violently. Cook, without stirring, until the caramelized sugar has liquefied again and the mixture is very smooth and a deep golden brown, 3 to 4 minutes. Remove the pan from the heat.

While whisking, slowly add 1 to 1 $1/2$ cups of the hot caramel to the egg yolk mixture to temper it. Add the remaining caramel, then pour the mixture back into the pan and cook over medium heat, stirring constantly with a plastic spatula, until the pudding begins to thicken and just comes to a boil, about 3 minutes. Immediately transfer the pudding to a mixing bowl, and whisk until smooth. Add the butter and let stand for 2 to 3 minutes before stirring, then stir until all of the butter has melted and the pudding is smooth.

Divide the macerated strawberries among six wineglasses or serving dishes. Pour the warm pudding over the strawberries, and refrigerate until well chilled. Serve cold, topped with softly whipped cream and garnished with mint sprigs.

White Chocolate and Lemon Pôts de Crème

Serves 6

3 cups half-and-half
Finely grated zest of 1 lemon
$1/2$ vanilla bean, split in half lengthwise
8 large egg yolks
$1/2$ teaspoon lemon oil (optional)
$1/2$ cup sugar
6 ounces white chocolate, chopped
1 $1/2$ cups softly whipped cream, as accompaniment
$1/2$ cup shaved white chocolate, for garnish

Combine the half-and-half, lemon zest, and vanilla bean in a heavy saucepan over medium heat and bring just to a boil. Remove the pan from the heat, cover, and set aside.

In a large metal bowl, whisk together the egg yolks, lemon oil, and sugar. Set the bowl over a pan of simmering water (make sure the bottom of the bowl does not touch the water), and cook, whisking constantly, just until the egg mixture is warm and the sugar is dissolved, 3 to 4 minutes. While whisking, slowly pour the egg yolk mixture into the warm half-and-half. Set the pan over medium heat and cook, whisking constantly, until the mixture coats the back of a spoon, about 5 minutes. Remove the pan from the heat. Remove and discard the vanilla bean. Add the white chocolate and let stand for a few minutes for the chocolate to melt, then whisk until smooth.

Divide the mixture among six coffee cups or 8-ounce ramekins, and refrigerate until chilled and set, at least 4 hours. Serve cold, topped with softly whipped cream and shaved white chocolate.

Brown Sugar Snow Eggs with Chocolate Crème Anglaise

Serves 6

CHOCOLATE CRÈME ANGLAISE
1 cup half-and-half
1 vanilla bean, split in half lengthwise
$1/2$ cup sugar
3 large egg yolks
6 ounces bittersweet chocolate, coarsely chopped
$1/4$ cup crème de cacao
Pinch of salt

BROWN SUGAR SNOW EGGS
6 egg whites
1 cup firmly packed dark brown sugar
Pinch of salt

$1/2$ cup shaved bittersweet chocolate, for garnish
Mint sprigs, for garnish

To prepare the crème anglaise, combine the half-and-half and vanilla bean in a heavy saucepan over low heat and bring just to a boil. Meanwhile, whisk together the sugar and egg yolks in a large bowl. When the half-and-half is hot, slowly whisk 1 to 1 $1/2$ cups of the half-and-half into the egg yolk mixture to temper it, or bring it up to the same temperature. Whisk the warm egg yolks into the remaining half-and-half, then cook over medium heat, whisking often, just until the sauce coats the back of a spoon, 4 to 5 minutes. Remove the pan from the heat. Remove and discard the vanilla bean. Add the chocolate, crème de cacao, and salt. Let the custard stand for a few minutes to melt the chocolate, then stir. Refrigerate until you are ready to serve dessert.

To prepare the snow eggs, in the clean bowl of a mixer fitted with the whip attachment, whip the egg whites on high speed until very frothy. While beating, add the brown sugar, about 1 tablespoon at a time, and beat until the sugar is dissolved. Add the salt and continue beating until the egg whites are very shiny and hold a stiff peak.

Meanwhile, in a stockpot over high heat, bring about 8 cups of water to a boil, then decrease the heat and simmer. Using two large serving spoons, form about $1/2$ cup of the egg white mixture into an egg shape and carefully slip it into the simmering water; continue forming and adding as many eggs as will fit in the pan without overcrowding. Cook for about 1 minute, then flip and cook 1 minute longer. Remove with a slotted spoon and drain on paper towels. Continue with the remaining egg white mixture.

To serve, ladle about $1/4$ cup of the custard sauce onto each plate and top with 2 snow eggs. Garnish with shaved chocolate and mint sprigs. Serve immediately.

Honey Custard

Serves 6

3 cups half-and-half
6 large eggs
$^{1}/_{2}$ cup sugar
$^{2}/_{3}$ cup honey
$^{1}/_{2}$ teaspoon pure vanilla extract
Pinch of salt
1 cup softly whipped cream, as accompaniment
Spice Sable Cookies (page 168), as accompaniment

Preheat the oven to 300°F.

Whisk together the half-and-half and eggs in a large bowl. Add the sugar, honey, vanilla extract, and salt, and mix well. Divide the custard among six 8-ounce ramekins. Set the ramekins in a shallow roasting pan, and fill the pan with enough hot water to reach about halfway up the sides of the ramekins. Carefully set the pan in the oven and bake the custards just until set, about 50 minutes, or until a knife inserted in the custards comes out clean. Remove the ramekins from the water bath. Let cool until tepid, then refrigerate until well chilled, about 2 hours.

Serve cold with softly whipped cream and Spice Sable Cookies.

Basics and Techniques

Fresh Bread Crumbs

Makes about 2 cups

5 slices rustic white bread

Preheat the oven to 350°F. Remove the crusts from the bread and discard. Tear the bread into pieces, place them in a food processor, and process to fine crumbs. Place the crumbs on a sheet pan and toast for about 10 minutes, or until golden brown.

Crostini

Makes 20 to 24 crostini

1 loaf French bread, cut into $1/4$-inch thick slices
$1/4$ cup extra virgin olive oil

Preheat the oven to 350°F. Lightly drizzle bread with olive oil, and arrange the slices on a sheet pan. Bake for about 15 minutes, or until golden brown.

Cornbread

Makes 1 8-inch square loaf

1 cup finely ground cornmeal
1 cup all purpose flour
1 teaspoon baking powder
$3/4$ teaspoon salt
$1/2$ teaspoon baking soda
$1/2$ cup buttermilk
$1/2$ cup milk
2 large eggs
2 tablespoons vegetable oil
2 tablespoons brown sugar

Preheat the oven to 375°F. Butter an 8-inch square pan. Combine the cornmeal, flour, baking powder, salt, and baking soda in a large bowl and mix well. In another bowl, whisk together the buttermilk, milk, eggs, oil, and brown sugar. Fold the wet ingredients into the dry ingredients and mix just until smooth. Pour the batter into the prepared pan. Bake for 25 to 30 minutes, or until a knife inserted in the cornbread comes out clean. Let the cornbread cool in the pan for about 5 minutes, then remove it from the pan. Serve warm.

Crème Fraîche

Makes about 2 cups

2 cups heavy whipping cream
2 tablespoons sour cream

181

In a small bowl, whisk together the whipping cream and sour cream. Cover and let sit at room temperature for 8 hours or overnight, then refrigerate until thickened. Refrigerated, the crème fraîche will keep for up to 1 week.

John's Secret Cure

Makes about 4 cups

2 cups firmly packed dark brown sugar
1 cup kosher salt
3 tablespoons ground mace
3 tablespoons ground allspice
3 tablespoons onion powder
3 tablespoons garlic powder
1 1/2 tablespoons ground cloves

Combine all the ingredients in a food processor and process until well blended. Store for up to six months in the refrigerator.

Mascarpone

Makes about 2 cups

2 cups heavy whipping cream
1 teaspoon tartaric acid (available at home winemaking supply shops)

In a saucepan over high heat, whisk together the cream and tartaric acid, and bring just to a boil. Remove the pan from the heat and let cool for about 10 minutes. Transfer the mixture to a strainer lined with several layers of cheesecloth, set the strainer over a bowl, and let the mixture sit in the refrigerator overnight. Remove the chilled mascarpone from the cheesecloth, and refrigerate it until you are ready to use it (discard the liquid in the bowl). The mascarpone will keep for 2 weeks.

Quick Puff Pastry

Makes about 3 1/2 pounds

4 1/2 cups all-purpose flour, plus more for folding process
2 cups unsalted butter, diced
1 teaspoon salt
1 cup plus 2 tablespoons cold water

Combine the flour, butter, and salt in a large bowl. Using your fingertips, mix the butter with the flour until it resembles a coarse meal (it's all right if there are some large pieces of butter). Add about 1 cup of the water and mix with a fork just until it comes together.

Transfer the dough to a well-floured board and form it into a rough rectangle. Fold one-third of the dough toward the center. Fold the other third over toward the center. Turn the dough 90 degrees. Sprinkle the dough with flour and roll it out into a 20 by 6-inch rectangle. Fold the dough in thirds again. Turn it 90 degrees, sprinkle with flour, and roll it out again. Repeat the process two more times.

Cover the dough with plastic wrap and refrigerate for at least 1 hour. Use as directed. (The dough can be cut into smaller pieces, wrapped, and kept frozen for up to 6 months.)

Cooked Basmati Rice

Makes about 4 cups

2 cups basmati rice or long-grain rice
1 tablespoon vegetable oil
3 cloves garlic, chopped
3 teaspoons peeled, chopped fresh ginger
4 cups chicken stock (page 184) or vegetable stock (page 186)
Salt and freshly ground black pepper

Preheat the oven to 350°F. Rinse the rice in a sieve under cold running water until the water runs clear; drain well.

Heat the oil in an ovenproof saucepan over high heat until very hot. Add the garlic and ginger, and sauté for 2 minutes. Add the rice, stir to coat it well with the oil, and sauté for about 2 minutes. Add the stock and season well with salt and pepper. Bring the mixture to a boil, cover the pan with a lid, and place it in the oven. Bake for 15 minutes. Stir well, cover, and bake until the rice is tender, about 15 minutes longer. Serve warm.

Cooked Wild Rice

Makes 4 cups

2 cups wild rice
6 cups water, or more as needed
Salt

Combine the rice and water in a large saucepan over high heat, season with salt, and bring to a boil. Decrease the heat to medium and simmer uncovered, adding more water to cover the rice as needed, until the rice is tender, 30 to 40 minutes. Drain well. Serve warm, or let cool and use as directed.

Simple Risotto

Makes about 3 cups

2 teaspoons extra virgin olive oil
2 cloves garlic, minced
1 cup arborio rice
3 cups chicken stock (page 184) or vegetable stock (page 186), kept at a simmer
Salt and freshly ground black pepper

Heat the oil in a large saucepan over medium-high heat until hot. Add the garlic and sauté for about 1 minute. Add the rice and sauté until the rice becomes opaque, 2 to 3 minutes. Add enough of the hot stock to just cover the rice, about 2 cups, and cook, stirring constantly, until the stock has been absorbed, about 4 minutes. Add another $1/2$ cup stock and continue cooking, stirring constantly, until the stock has been absorbed, about 4 minutes. Continue adding the stock, 1 cup at a time, and cooking until all of the stock has been absorbed and the rice is al dente, about 20 minutes total. Season to taste with salt and pepper. Serve warm, or use as directed.

Fish Stock

Makes about 8 cups

3 pounds fish bones (use bones from white-fleshed fish only), coarsely chopped

2 tablespoons unsalted butter

4 leeks, white part only, rinsed well and coarsely chopped

4 large onions, coarsely chopped

4 stalks celery, coarsely chopped

4 cloves garlic, chopped

$^1/_2$ cup mushroom stems

2 cups dry white wine

8 sprigs thyme

16 cups cold water

In a large bowl or stockpot, cover the bones with cold water and soak for 1 to 2 hours to remove any remaining traces of blood. Drain.

Heat the butter in a large stockpot over high heat until melted and bubbling. Add the leeks, onions, celery, garlic, and mushroom stems, and sauté for 3 to 4 minutes. Add the wine and bones, decrease the heat to medium-low, cover the pot, and sweat the mixture for about 8 minutes. Add the thyme and water and simmer, uncovered, for 25 minutes. Strain through a fine sieve into a bowl and use immediately, or let cool to room temperature before refrigerating. The stock will keep refrigerated for up to 1 week, or frozen for up to 6 months.

Chicken or Turkey Stock

Makes about 8 cups

4 pounds chicken or turkey bones, rinsed

4 onions, coarsely chopped

4 carrots, coarsely chopped

4 stalks celery, coarsely chopped

6 cloves garlic, chopped

8 sprigs thyme

16 cups water

2 bay leaves

In a large stockpot over high heat, combine the bones, onions, carrots, celery, garlic, thyme, and water, and bring just to a boil. Add the bay leaves, decrease the heat to low, and simmer for 4 to 6 hours, or until the stock is richly flavored. Strain through a fine sieve into a bowl and use immediately, or let cool to room temperature before refrigerating. The stock will keep refrigerated for up to 1 week, or frozen for up to 6 months.

Note: To make rich chicken or turkey stock, reduce the stock over high heat until about 5 cups remain and the flavor has intensified.

Lamb Stock

Makes about 4 cups

5 pounds lamb bones
2 onions, coarsely chopped
1 carrot, coarsely chopped
3 stalks celery, coarsely chopped
3 cloves garlic, chopped
2 tablespoons tomato paste
1 cup dry white wine
8 cups water
1 bay leaf

Preheat the oven to 450°F. Place the bones, onions, carrot, celery, and garlic in a roasting pan, and roast for about 1 hour, or until the bones turn golden brown. Spread the tomato paste over the mixture and roast for 10 minutes longer. Transfer the mixture to a large stockpot. Add the wine to the roasting pan and, using a wooden spoon, scrape the bottom of the pan to deglaze. Pour the wine liquid into the stockpot. Add the water and the bay leaf. Bring to a boil over high heat. Decrease the heat to low and simmer for 6 to 8 hours, or until the stock is richly flavored. Strain through a fine sieve and use immediately, or let cool to room temperature before refrigerating. The stock will keep refrigerated for up to 1 week, or frozen for up to 6 months.

Mushroom Stock

Makes about 4 cups

1 ounce dried mushrooms
6 cups white mushrooms
2 carrots, coarsely chopped
4 stalks celery, coarsely chopped
2 onions, coarsely chopped
6 cloves garlic
6 sprigs herbs, such as thyme, basil, or marjoram
8 cups cold water

Combine all of the ingredients in a large stockpot over high heat, and bring to a boil. Decrease the heat to low and simmer for 4 to 5 hours, adding additional cold water as needed, until the stock is richly flavored. Strain through a fine sieve into a large saucepan, and cook over medium heat until reduced by about half. Use immediately, or let cool to room temperature before refrigerating. The stock will keep refrigerated for up to 1 week, or frozen for up to 6 months.

Vegetable Stock

Makes about 8 cups

6 onions, coarsely chopped
8 carrots, coarsely chopped
10 stalks celery, coarsely chopped
8 ounces mushrooms, coarsely chopped
8 cloves garlic, chopped
6 shallots, chopped
12 sprigs thyme
16 cups water

In a large stockpot over high heat, combine the onions, carrots, celery, mushrooms, garlic, shallots, thyme, and water. Bring just to a boil. Decrease the heat and simmer for about 1 hour, or until the stock is very flavorful. Strain through a fine sieve into a bowl and use immediately, or let cool to room temperature before refrigerating. The stock will keep refrigerated for up to 1 week, or frozen for up to 6 months.

Note: To make roasted vegetable stock, place all the vegetables in a large baking dish and roast in a 425°F oven for 20 minutes. Add the roasted vegetables to the stockpot of boiling water and proceed as directed above.

Veal or Beef Stock

Makes about 8 cups

10 pounds veal or beef bones
4 onions, coarsely chopped
2 carrots, coarsely chopped
6 stalks celery, coarsely chopped
6 cloves garlic, chopped
4 tablespoons tomato paste
2 cups dry red wine
16 cups water
2 bay leaves

Preheat the oven to 450°F. Combine the bones, onions, carrots, celery, and garlic in a roasting pan, and roast for about 1 hour, or until the bones are well browned. Spread the tomato paste over the mixture and roast for 10 minutes longer. Transfer the mixture to a large stockpot. Add the wine to the roasting pan and scrape the bottom of the pan to deglaze. Pour the wine mixture into the stockpot. Add the water and bay leaf, and bring to a boil over high heat. Decrease the heat to low and simmer for 6 to 8 hours, until the stock is richly flavored. Strain through a fine sieve into a bowl and use immediately, or let cool to room temperature before refrigerating. The stock will keep refrigerated for up to 1 week, or frozen for up to 6 months.

TECHNIQUES

Cooking Black-Eyed Peas

Place dried black-eyed peas in a large bowl, add enough cold water to cover, and let them soak overnight; drain. Transfer the beans to a large saucepan, and add enough cold water to cover. Bring to a boil over medium-high heat. Decrease the heat to low and simmer the black-eyed peas until tender, about 45 minutes to 1 hour. Drain well.

Cooking Cannellini Beans

Place dried cannellini beans in a large bowl, add enough cold water to cover, and let them soak overnight; drain. Transfer the beans to a large saucepan, and add enough cold water to cover. Bring to a boil over medium-high heat. Decrease the heat to low and simmer the beans until tender, about 1 hour. Drain well.

Cooking Chickpeas

Place dried chickpeas in a large bowl, add enough cold water to cover, and let them soak overnight; drain. Transfer the chickpeas to a large saucepan, and add enough cold water to cover. Bring to a boil over medium-high heat, then drain. Again add enough cold water to cover. Bring to a boil over medium-high heat. Decrease the heat to low and simmer the chickpeas until tender, about 1 hour. Drain well.

Roasting Bell Peppers and Fresh Chiles

Preheat the broiler. Place the peppers or chiles on a baking sheet and broil, turning until the skins are evenly blistered and charred, about 15 minutes. Transfer to a bowl, cover with plastic wrap, and set aside to cool. When the peppers or chiles are cool enough to handle, peel off the skins, remove the stems, and wipe the seeds away. Do not rinse the peppers or chiles under running water because this washes away much of the roasted flavor. Use as directed, or drizzle with olive oil and store in an airtight container in the refrigerator for up to 2 months.

Roasting and Pulverizing Dried Chiles

Preheat the oven to 350°F. Place the dried chiles on a sheet pan and roast until puffy and dark brown, about 12 minutes. Let cool. Remove and discard the stems and seeds. Using a coffee or spice grinder, grind the chiles to a fine powder. Store the powder in an airtight container for up to 1 month.

Shaving Chocolate

Run a sharp vegetable peeler along a bar of chocolate to shave off curls.

Toasting Coconut

Preheat the oven to 350°F. Spread the shredded coconut on a sheet pan. Bake for about 5 minutes, stir, and then bake 5 to 7 minutes longer, until golden brown. Let cool completely on the pan. Keep in an airtight container for up to 5 days.

Roasting Garlic

Preheat the oven to 250°F. Slice about $1/4$ inch off the top of each garlic head and discard. Drizzle each garlic head with 2 tablespoons extra virgin olive oil and wrap tightly in aluminum foil. Roast for 40 to 50 minutes, until soft. Squeeze each clove to remove the roasted garlic from the papery outer layer. Roasted garlic will keep in the refrigerator for 2 to 3 weeks.

Blanching and Shocking Green Beans

Bring a stockpot of water to a boil over high heat. Add the beans and cook until crisp-tender. Drain immediately and transfer to a large bowl of ice water to stop the cooking process. Use as directed.

Frenching a Rack of Lamb

Using the back of a knife, scrape the bones on the rack to remove the excess fat. Using the blade of the knife, cut off any extra fat from the bottom of the bones.

Toasting Nuts or Seeds

Preheat the oven to 350°F. Place the nuts (whole or ground) or seeds on a baking sheet and toast in a 350°F oven for about 10 minutes, or until golden brown and aromatic. Let cool completely, then use as directed.

Peeling Peaches

Bring a stockpot of water to a boil. Cut an x in the bottom of each peach. Add the whole peaches to the stockpot and blanch briefly, about 1 minute. Using a slotted spoon, immediately transfer the peaches to a large bowl of ice water. When the peaches are cool, peel them. The skins should slip off easily.

Cooking Red Potatoes

Scrub small red potatoes and combine them in a saucepan with enough cold water to cover. Bring to a boil over high heat. Decrease the heat to medium and simmer until the potatoes are tender, about 15 minutes. Drain well. Serve warm, or let cool and use as directed. Two pounds of potatoes will serve six as a side dish.

Roasting Shallots

Preheat the oven to 250°F. Place the shallots in a small baking dish or ovenproof sauté pan, drizzle with extra virgin olive oil, using $1/4$ cup oil for every 6 shallots. Roast for 40 to 50 minutes, until soft. Roasted shallots will keep in the refrigerator for up to 2 weeks.

Toasting Spices

Heat a dry skillet over medium-high heat until hot. Add the whole or ground spices and toast while stirring continuously. Toast whole spices for 3 to 5 minutes; toast ground spices for about 2 minutes, or until lightly browned and aromatic.

Seeding Tomatoes

Cut the tomatoes in half crosswise. Cup one tomato half in the palm of your hand and gently squeeze until the seeds spill out.

Glossary

Arugula: Also called rocket, arugula is a tender green with a nutty, spicy flavor. I like to add it to salads, sandwiches, and pastas.

Asian chile sauce: A sauce made with chiles and garlic.

Blanch: To partially cook briefly in boiling water.

Bok choy (and baby bok choy): Also called Chinese white cabbage, bok choy is a dark green cabbage that somewhat resembles Swiss chard; baby bok choy is a smaller, more tender variety.

Caramelize: To cook sugar or an ingredient with a naturally high sugar content (such as some vegetables and meats) over high heat to brown the natural sugars and develop a deeper flavor.

Chickpea flour: A fine flour made from dried chickpeas.

Chile paste: A Chinese condiment made from fermented fava beans, red chiles, and sometimes, garlic.

Chipotle chiles in adobo sauce: Canned smoked jalapeño peppers in a thick, spicy sauce. Available in specialty stores and most grocery stores.

Crème fraîche: Cream combined with sour cream (or buttermilk) that is left out at room temperature for 8 to 24 hours, then refrigerated until thickened.

Crystallized ginger: Also known as candied ginger. Available in most grocery stores and in Asian markets.

Curry paste: A mixture of ghee (clarified butter), vinegar, and curry powder used to flavor Indian and Asian dishes. Sold in gourmet and specialty shops.

Emulsify: To completely blend together an oil or fat with an acid such as vinegar or lemon juice.

Herbes de Provence: A mixture of dried herbs, usually thyme, rosemary, bay, lavender, savory, and basil.

Instant sour paste: A potent Asian flavoring paste that adds complexity to many dishes. I prefer the Tom Yum brand, which I use like salt and pepper. It keeps indefinitely in the refrigerator.

Julienne: To cut into matchsticks about $1/8$ inch across by 2 inches long.

Kalamata olives: Smooth-skinned, dark purple, brine-cured Greek olives with an intense taste.

Kosher salt: Pure salt with an even, coarse texture; more soluble than table salt. Available in specialty markets and most supermarkets.

Lemongrass: A standard herb in Vietnamese and Thai cooking. Use fresh lemongrass for cooking; dried lemongrass is mainly used for tea. Available in Asian markets and some grocery stores.

Lemon olive oil: Extra virgin olive oil pressed with lemons. Available in gourmet markets.

Mesclun: Mixed wild salad greens.

Mirin: Sweet Japanese rice wine used for cooking.

Nonreactive bowl/pan/container: Made of glass, ceramic, or stainless steel. Metal components in aluminum and cast-iron can react with the acids in ingredients resulting in an off flavor.

Oil-cured tomatoes: Unlike sun-dried tomatoes, which are completely dried, oil-cured tomatoes are partially dried before being packed in olive oil with garlic and herbs. Available in gourmet markets and some grocery stores.

Orange oil: Essential oil from the skin of oranges.

Pancetta: Unsmoked, peppered Italian bacon. Available in gourmet markets.

Panko: Dry, untoasted Japanese breadcrumbs with a coarse, crispy texture.

Parchment paper: Oil- and moisture-resistant paper used to line baking sheets and pans to prevent baked items from sticking.

Plum vinegar: A type of vinegar made from plums. Available in specialty stores and some grocery stores.

Prosciutto: Dry-cured, spiced Italian ham available in gourmet markets.

Reduce: To thicken and intensify the flavor of a sauce by boiling it down.

Shock: To submerge briefly in ice-cold water to stop the cooking process.

Smoked paprika: A Spanish paprika made with smoked chile peppers.

Sweet-hot chile sauce: A sauce made with chiles, garlic, sugar, and vinegar. Available at Asian markets and most grocery stores.

Sweet soy sauce: A sweet, syrup-like Indonesian soy sauce; also called kecap manis.

Tahini: A paste made from toasted sesame seeds that is used in Middle Eastern cooking.

Tamarind concentrate: Sweet-sour paste made from the fruit of the pods of the tamarind tree.

Tapenade: A thick paste made from capers, anchovies, black olives, olive oil, and lemon juice.

Wild mushrooms: All edible, nonpoisonous mushrooms that are indigenous to certain areas throughout the Pacific Northwest, among other regions. Some of the most common are chanterelles, enoki, morels, and shiitakes, which are all known for their particularly earthy qualities.

Index

Caprial's Bistro-Style Cuisine

Caprial's Soups and Sandwiches

Caprial Cooks for Friends

Caprial's Desserts